Nelson Grammar

F R Witty

Revision Book 5

Thomas Nelson and Sons Ltd
Nelson House   Mayfield Road
Walton-on-Thames   Surrey
KT12 5PL   UK

51 York Place
Edinburgh
EH1 3JD   UK

Thomas Nelson (Hong Kong) Ltd
Toppan Building 10/F
22A Westlands Road
Quarry Bay   Hong Kong

Distributed in Australia by
Thomas Nelson Australia
480 La Trobe Street
Melbourne   Victoria 3000
and in Sydney, Brisbane, Adelaide and Perth

© F.R. Witty 1980
First published by Thomas Nelson and Sons Ltd 1980

ISBN 0-17-424385-5
NPN 9 8 7 6

Printed in Hong Kong

Filmset by Vantage Photosetting Company Limited Southampton

**The publishers wish to thank the following
who have kindly given permission for
the use of copyright material:
Jonathan Cape Limited and the Arthur Ransome
Estate for extract from *Swallows and Amazons*
by Arthur Ransome; Ernest Benn for extract
from the *Wombles Book* by Elisabeth Beresford.**

Contents

Introduction

A knowledge of the basic rules of the English language – that is to say its grammar – is essential if you are to write and speak well.

In Book 5 of *Nelson Grammar* you will find a complete summary of the rules dealt with in Books 1–4, and some rules are considered at a more advanced level.

Book 5 tells you about common mistakes in writing and speaking, and how to avoid them. It tells you about styles of writing – how to write a letter or a good essay, how to form paragraphs, how to take notes and write from notes, and the forms of poetry and rhyme.

Each topic is dealt with concisely in a box. After you have read this carefully, there are exercises to give you confidence in mastering the topic. At the end of each section there are revision exercises for further practice.

Please do not write any of the answers to the exercises in this book. Use paper or an exercise book.

Nouns

A noun is the name of any person or thing

It may be the name of something you can touch or see.

tree hill man table

pen daisy Mary

Peter

It may be the name of something you cannot touch or see.

love hate pain

truth morning

June

A

1 Write the names of five things which you can see in the street.

2 Write the names of five things which you cannot touch or see.

B Write the names of four different things under each of these headings.

1 in a greengrocer's shop

2 indoor games to play

3 outdoor games

4 toys

5 birds

6 animals

7 fish

8 boys' names

9 girls' names

10 garden tools

11 things in a kitchen

12 countries

C Copy this crossword and fill in the words from the clues. All the words are nouns.

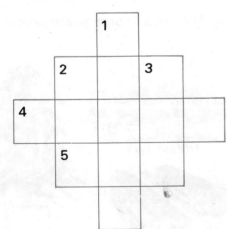

Clues

Across:

2 A boy may wear this on his head.
4 A girl becomes this when she grows up.
5 A place full of lions.

Down:

1 An animal which travels across the desert.
2 A fish which lives in the sea.
3 We cook things in this.

5

Proper and common nouns

A noun which is the name of a particular place, person or thing is called a proper noun. It always begins with a capital letter.

David Copperfield   Monday

Roy Rogers   Dorset Road

Marks and Spencer

A noun which refers to something of *is the name of that* which there are many different *has* examples is called a common noun. It *lots of* only begins with a capital letter if it is the first word in a sentence.

book   day   road   man   shop

A   Write the proper nouns from this list. Make their first letters capitals.

penknife   author   dover   whale   arthur ransome   sausage

buckingham palace   steady   sir terence bond   driver   top

badger   windmill road   party   grafton street   tim o'donnelly

B   Write these passages, putting in capital letters where needed.

1   marie curie was a polish scientist who, in the year 1898, discovered the chemical element radium. she worked in paris and in 1910 wrote 'a treatise on radioactivity'. she became a professor at the sorbonne university in paris, where she died in 1934.

2   george stephenson made the first steam locomotive for the stockton–darlington railway in 1825. he made other locomotives, including the rocket, for the manchester–liverpool line in 1830.

C   Arrange these jumbled letters to make nouns. The ones in orange are proper nouns. Make their first letters capitals.

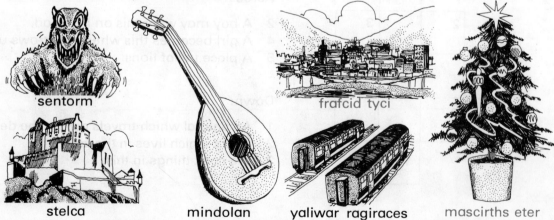

sentorm

frafcid tyci

stelca

mindolan

yaliwar ragiraces

mascirths eter

Collective nouns

A collective noun is the name of a group of people or things all of one kind.

Examples: a flock of sheep

a herd of cows

a bunch of grapes

A Write the phrases below, choosing a collective noun from the box to fill each space.

| swarm litter plague bunch clump pack galaxy shoal band herd |

1 a ——— of locusts

2 a ——— of flowers

3 a ——— of puppies

4 a ——— of musicians

5 a ——— of wolves

6 a ——— of fish

7 a ——— of elephants

8 a ——— of stars

9 a ——— of trees

10 a ——— of bees

B Write this passage. Use collective nouns to fill the spaces.

A ——— of people was pouring into the local football ground to see two ——— of players competing for the cup. A ——— of birds circled overhead. The mayoress was to present the cup, and she received a ——— of flowers. The ——— was restless with excitement and small boys were chatting and jumping about like a ——— of monkeys. Then the teams ran out from the dressing room up a ——— of steps and the game began.

C Write the collective noun for these.

Compound nouns

A compound noun is a noun formed by joining two nouns together.

Examples:

A **matchbox** is a box for matches.

A **tablecloth** is a cloth for a table.

A Make fifteen compound nouns from this list by joining any two suitable nouns together.

arm	board	cow	house	light	room	boy	mat
ball	bottle	cup	jam	man	spoon	brush	milk
bird	card	door	lamp	paper	tea	foot	tooth
black	chair	egg	life	pot	table	guard	wall

B Find twelve compound nouns in this passage.

Dai Rees was the goalkeeper for the school football team. His mother was a schoolteacher, and she always made him do his homework properly. He lived in the schoolhouse and walked to school each day along the footpath on the hillside. He liked looking after the greenhouse at home, and growing plants in his own flowerbed. His father had four beehives and showed Dai how to lift out the honeycombs and extract the honey, which was stored in honeypots.

C Write a compound noun to name each of these pictures.

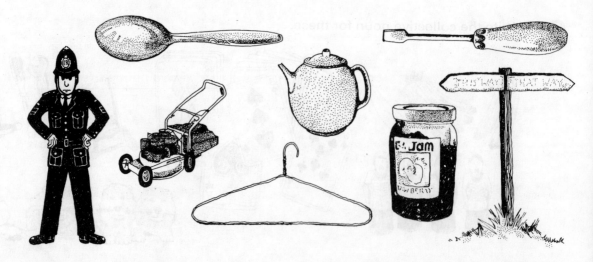

Nouns made from verbs

Many nouns are made from verbs.

Examples:

From the verb **run** we get:

Phil scores thirty **runs** at cricket.

Jill is a good **runner**.

Donald's **running** is better than his jumping.

manage → **manager**   **manageress**   **management**

enter → **entrant**   **entrance**   **entry**

recite → **reciter**   **recital**   **recitation**

There are often changes in spelling when we make nouns from verbs.

Example:

thieve → **thief theft**

Always look up the word in your dictionary if you are not sure.

A   Write all the nouns you can make from each of these verbs.

rebel   try   cut   explain   propose   hate   act   clothe   occupy   examine

B   Write these sentences, putting a noun made from the verb in brackets in the space.

1   The prisoner had a fair ———. (try)

2   Drake sailed on a voyage of ———. (explore)

3   The flies caused us a lot of ———. (irritate)

4   Your ——— is only a slight one. (injure)

5   Shouts of ——— greeted the clown. (laugh)

6   The ——— had to leave the competition. (lose)

C   Write a verb describing each picture, and then make two nouns from each verb.

Plurals of common nouns

A singular noun refers to one person or thing. **table   house**

A plural noun refers to more than one thing. **tables   houses**

There are several ways of making plural nouns.

1   Add **s**.   **forks   trees   cats**

2   Add **es** when the noun ends in **ch**, **s**, **sh** or **x**.   **churches   buses   foxes**

3   When the noun ends in **y** with no vowel before it, change the **y** to **ies**.
ladies   canaries   babies

4   When the noun ends in **f** or **fe**, change it to **ves**.   **leaves   thieves
loaves   knives**

Exceptions are   **chief – chiefs,   dwarf – dwarfs,   roof – roofs,   safe –
safes.**

A   Write these sentences, choosing the correct plural from the brackets.

1   How many ——— did you buy? (loafs   loaves)

2   There are ——— on the sands. (donkies   donkeys)

3   Put the books on the ———. (shelves   shelfs)

4   We could hear the ——— singing. (canarys   canaries)

B   Write plural nouns to fit these meanings.

1   Small horses

2   Used to cut food

3   Used to sweep the floor

4   A lot of money may be kept in them.

5   Animals that hunt in packs

6   Low areas between hills

C   Write plural nouns to fit these pictures.

5 Some nouns ending in **o** form the plural by adding **s**.   **cellos**   **curios**
dynamos   **Eskimos**   **radios**   **solos**
Others add **es**.   **cargoes**   **dominoes**   **echoes**   **heroes**
potatoes   **tomatoes**

6 The plurals of some compound nouns are formed by making the first word plural.   **men-at-arms**   **passers-by**

7 Some nouns change to the plural by a change in the word.   **man–men**
foot–feet   **tooth–teeth**   **goose–geese**   **child–children**   **ox–oxen**

8 Some nouns do not change in the plural.   **bison**   **deer**   **moose**
cod   **mackerel**   **trout**   **salmon**   **sheep**

9 Some nouns are always plural.   **overalls**   **trousers**   **shorts**   **pliers**
scissors   **spectacles**

But a **pair of trousers** is singular.

A The plurals in orange in this passage are wrong. Write the passage again correctly.

A Canadian trapper, with some Eskimoes, set out to hunt wild mooses and deers, and to catch salmons and trouts in the rivers. They had radioes so that they could talk with those at home. They shot some wild reindeers, and some gooses which flew overhead. There are no bisons to be seen in this part of North America, but along the coast they did meet some fishermen bringing back their cargos of cods and mackerels.

B Write this passage, putting each noun in orange in the plural.

Two lady went shopping in the country for loaf, potato and other necessity. They passed two church on the way to the village. They saw the roof of the house still covered with snow which had fallen some day ago. As they turned a corner in the lane, a couple of fox ran across. Huntsman rode after them in pursuit, jumping across hedge and ditch as they went, watched by the passer-by. Then the sound of hoof died away, and the two lady and the onlooker walked on.

C Write plural nouns to fit these pictures.

Plurals of proper nouns

There are three rules for forming the plurals of proper nouns.

1 Add **es** if the proper noun ends in **s** unless it sounds very odd.

2 Add **es** if the noun ends in **ss**, **ch**, **sh** or **x**.

3 In all other cases add **s**.

Examples:

We last went to France two Julys ago.

In the race between the Mercury and Mercedes cars, the Mercurys won the team prize, and the Mercedes came a close second.

The Joneses, Roberts and Coxes are all going to the concert, but the Mosses, Nashes, Wolfes, Lightfoots, Whitemans, Goodchilds and Metcalfs are not going.

A   Write these sentences, choosing the correct plural from the brackets. Some are common nouns.

1   The ——— are coming for tea. (Berries   Berrys)

2   Will the ——— be there? (Jones   Joneses)

3   The ——— are a happy family. (Birches   Birchs)

4   What a lot of ——— are on the trees. (berries   berrys)

5   The ——— are all closed today. (laundrys   laundries)

6   The last two ——— have been very cold. (Januaries   Januarys)

7   There are two ——— in our class. (Henrys   Henries)

8   We had some Banbury apples and some Worcesters, but the ——— were riper. (Banburys   Banburies)

9   My neighbour keeps budgerigars and ———. (canarys   canaries)

10   Are you going to invite the ———? (Wilcoxs   Wilcoxes)

B   Write the plural of each of these nouns. Some are common nouns, but those with a capital letter are proper nouns.

box   deer   Mercedes   piccolo   penny   February   café   domino

mackerel   gulf   mattress   Proudfoot   circus   taxi   hero   trolley   church

bison   Billy   Fox

Possessive nouns

An apostrophe **'** is used to show ownership. When it is added to a noun, the word is called a possessive noun. For a singular noun, add **s** after the apostrophe unless the noun already ends in **s**.

Examples: the ostrich's eggs
Mr Jones' house

For a plural noun put the apostrophe after the **s**.

Example: the twins' uncle

If the plural noun does not end in **s**, add **s**.

Example: the children's games

A Change these nouns into possessive nouns.

sheep lady ladies man men church churches deer buses Wendy

B Put an apostrophe in the right places in these sentences.

1 The boys coats were soaked after the days rain.

2 The passengers tickets were punched at the platforms entrance.

3 Only ticket holders were admitted to the clubs ground.

4 The Roberts friends arrived five minutes later.

5 The cows milk was kept in the farmers churns.

6 We sit for our examinations in three days time.

7 The days work consisted of lifting the farmers potatoes.

8 Stanleys shoes are badly worn.

C Use possessive nouns to describe these pictures.

Example:

the torches' batteries

Think back

A Make two lists of the nouns in this passage, headed COMMON NOUNS and PROPER NOUNS.

Trevor, his sister Samantha, and their parents lived in a new house. The house, in Crompton Road, Newborough, was one that had just been built on the Sunglow housing estate. There were many other houses being built all around. Bricklayers were laying bricks. Joiners were sawing planks and making window frames. Mr Stone and his team of slaters were laying slates on the framework of the roofs. Mr Lead the plumber and Mr Sparks the electrician, with their men, were putting pipes and electric wires in the houses. There was bustle and activity everywhere.

B Write this passage. Choose a collective noun from the box to fill each space.

gang	sheaves	team	brood
chest	bench	flocks	litter

Ranjit was the son of a farmer who had a large farm in the country. He loved to go with the ——— of oxen which pulled his father's wagons. At harvest time he helped to stack the ——— of corn in the wagons. He liked to watch the ——— of birds wheeling overhead, and the antics of the ——— of puppies which had just been born. He also looked after a newly-hatched ——— of chicks.
One night a ——— of thieves broke into their house and stole some diamonds from a ——— of drawers in his parents' bedroom. The thieves were caught and brought before a ——— of magistrates.

C Make as many compound nouns as you can by joining any two suitable nouns together.

sun fire house fly shade cup spoon tea light corn butter
glasses field lamp table

D Make two nouns from each of these verbs, then write each one in a sentence.

manage inspect wait open serve lose sit plan beg try

E Write these nouns one underneath another, then opposite each noun write whether it is a common, proper or compound noun.

money lemonade Mr Twigg turnstile penny weasel Birmingham
coathook sausage furniture thrust Judy herring honesty vegetables
candlestick Africa butcher

F Copy this crossword and fill in the words from the clues. All the words are common nouns, except one. Which is the proper noun?

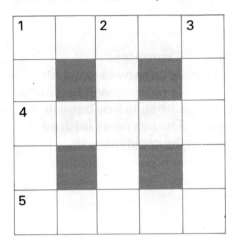

Clues

Across:

1 A short story with a moral
4 The opposite of 'left' or 'wrong'
5 A dog-like African animal, famous for its 'laugh'

Down

1 The river by the city of Edinburgh
2 A short brass wind instrument
3 An additional amount

G What are the plurals of these nouns?

cello   Eskimo   hoof   cod

child   Mercedes   shears   roof

H Use an apostrophe to shorten each of these phrases.

Example: a hockey team for ladies → a ladies' hockey team

1 the wool of the sheep
2 rifles for soldiers
3 thatched roofs of the cottages
4 icing of the cakes
5 spire of the church

Verbs

A verb is a word of doing, or action. It tells what is happening, or has happened or will happen.
Every sentence has a verb.

A sentence may only have a main verb like **is**, **was**, **walk**. Or it may consist of a main verb and an auxiliary like **has been**, **shall go** or **will be**.

Examples:
John **moves** the chair.
Tomorrow **will be** Friday.
Christine **has been** ill.
The man **was injured** in the accident.

A Make a list of the verbs in this passage.

In a gas explosion at Sheffield, eight houses were damaged and windows were shattered in houses across the road. One lady was asleep on the ground floor of her home when the explosion happened, blowing the roof off and starting a fire in the cellar. It is believed that it was caused by a main which fractured. Police sealed off the road and several people were evacuated. Temporary repairs were made by gas board officials.

B Write this passage. Use verbs from the box to fill the spaces. You will need to use some verbs more than once.

is   is played
was played
is strung   has
weighs   dates
were changed
stretches   covered

Tennis ——— a very old game, and ——— by kings and nobles in France and England in the 15th century. The modern game of Lawn Tennis ——— back to 1873, although the rules ——— in later years. The game ——— by two or four players. The net ——— across the middle of the court. The ball ——— a hollow rubber ball ——— with cloth, and ——— about 2 ounces or 57 grams. It ——— a diameter of about $2\frac{1}{2}$ inches or 6.4 centimetres. The racket ——— an oval frame and ——— with gut or nylon.

C There are seven verbs among this group of words. Find them, and write each verb in a sentence.

talk Sunday shall belief stew after accompany loss both accept knowledge should grief right consider

Auxiliary Verbs

The auxiliary or 'helper' verb is one added to the main verb.
There are primary auxiliaries like **do**, **have**, **be**, and modal auxiliaries like **can**, **must**, **may**, etc.
Do is used to form the negative and interrogative of verbs:

Examples: **Do** you understand?   He **did**n't go.

Be is used to form different tenses:

Examples: He **is** walking.   They **were** beaten.   He **will** go.

Have is used to form different tenses:

Examples: He **has** eaten.   He wondered what **had** happened.

A   Write this passage, underlining the auxiliary verbs.

There have been several bad fires in the town centre this week. The fire brigade has been called out several times and the police are investigating the matter. They believe someone is deliberately starting the fires.
   Jed Smith is talking to his neighbour about the fires:
"Did you see that big fire in the supermarket this morning?" he asked.
"Yes," said Pete, "it has caused a lot of damage and several people were injured in it. The police are looking into the matter and I hope they catch whoever is doing it."
"Don't worry," said Jed. "The police are following up all the clues and they will catch the culprit before the week is out."

B   Write these sentences, filling each blank with an auxiliary verb.

1   John———— not like tea. He prefers coffee.

2   ———— you finished the work you———— doing?

3   Mother———— hanging the clothes on the line.

4   The weather forecast says there———— be storms this evening.

5   The phone rang three times but Mary———— not answer it.

6   ———— you meet Anne when you———— shopping in town this morning?

7   The accident———— reported on the news but the police———— already informed William earlier that day.

Modal Auxiliaries

The modal auxiliaries affect the meaning of the main verb.

The modal auxiliaries are:

must have to need to	} express obligation	**Examples:** I **must** rest. I **have to** go out. I **need to** see a doctor.
can be able	} express ability	**Examples:** I **can** sing. I **am able** to swim.
can may	} express permission	**Examples:** You **can** go. **May** I sit down?
should ought to	} express moral obligation	**Examples:** I **ought to** visit her. I **should** work harder.

All modal auxiliaries are followed by the main verb in the infinitive,
e.g. You must **leave**.

A   Write the passage underlining all the auxiliary verbs.

Mary had to go to the hospital last week. She was playing netball when she tripped
and fell. "Oh dear, I can't get up. I think I have broken my ankle."
   "Don't move," said the teacher, "you may have only sprained it but we must get
you to the hospital at once."
   At the hospital the nurse bandaged Mary's ankle and she was given an injection.
"You should be more careful," said the nurse. "It's a pretty nasty sprain but you will
be able to walk on the leg again in a week's time."
   Now Mary is feeling a lot better. The doctor says she must rest the ankle for
another few days but that she can start practising netball again next week.

B   Write these sentences, filling each blank with an auxiliary verb.

1   It ———— snow so I think I ———— put on my overcoat.

2   Bob ———— not go out as he ———— not finished his homework.

3   We ———— leave now or we ———— be late.

4   ———— not open the window. It ———— raining.

Tense

The tense of a verb tells you when the action is taking place.
There are three main tenses.

What is happening now
is in the **present tense**.

Example:

Pam sees the ball.

What has happened is
in the **past tense**.

Example:

Pam saw the ball.

What is still to happen is
in the **future tense**.

Example:

Pam will see the ball.

A Here is a forecast of tomorrow's weather written in the future sense. Rewrite it in the past tense, after the weather changes have taken place.

Most of England and Wales will have rain, but there will be bright intervals. Northern England and Scotland will have sunny intervals and showers, and there will be snow on higher ground in Scotland. it will be cold and windy but a slow thaw will continue in most areas. The sunny intervals will be longer in the South. Winds will be north to north-west, moving to west during the day.

B Write these sentences, putting in the past tense of the verbs in the brackets.

1 Thomas Edison ——— the electric lamp in 1879. (invent)

2 Netball ——— in the United States in 1891. (originate)

3 The boy ——— the ball through the window. (kick)

4 I ——— ball with my friend yesterday. (play)

5 The horse ——— across the field. (gallop)

C Write these sentences, choosing the correct tense of the verb in brackets to fill each space.

1 We ——— the tickets tomorrow. (book)

2 Wilhelm Röntgen ——— X-rays in 1895. (discover)

3 The market ——— open every Friday. (be)

4 Sarah ——— to visit you next weekend. (come)

5 It ——— all day yesterday. (rain)

Past tense

The simple past tense is usually made by adding **d** or **ed** to the infinitive.

Examples:

It snowed.   I skated.   I tried.

When you make the past tense with an auxiliary, the past participle is used. The past participle is also usually made by adding **d** or **ed** to the infinitive.

Example: He said he had finished the game.

A   Write these sentences. Fill each space with the simple past tense of the verb in brackets.

1   They ——— for new members of the committee. (vote)

2   The police ——— the thieves' car. (chase)

3   The voters ——— a new councillor. (elect)

4   The rabbit ——— a raw carrot. (chew)

5   We ——— Max to join us. (persuade)

B   Write these sentences. Fill each space with either the past tense of the verb in brackets or an auxiliary and past participle.

1   Mark ——— at his new school yesterday. (start)

2   They ——— the meal by the time I arrived. (finish)

3   We ——— the shelves with books this morning. (fill)

4   I wish I ——— harder. (work)

C   Write this passage. Put the verbs in orange into the past tense.

John wants to see his friend Keith before the holiday ends. He telephones and asks him to come over. Keith arrives half an hour later and the two boys decide to go to the pictures. But they want to see different films and argue for some time before they finally decide to see 'Star Wars'.

Irregular verbs

Many verbs do not follow the rules for making the past tense and past participles.

Examples:

verb	begin	bring	fly	give	go	see	swim	write
past tense	began	brought	flew	gave	went	saw	swam	wrote
past participle	begun	brought	flown	given	gone	seen	swum	written

A Write the simple past tense of these verbs.

give   do   write   forget   catch   ride   hide   take   fly   drive   buy   eat

am   draw   leave   throw   ring   know

B Write these sentences, choosing the correct word from the brackets.

1   Have you (seen   seed) the film at the Odeon?

2   Joanne had (forgotten   forgetted) to bring her swimming costume.

3   We (swam   swum) three lengths yesterday.

4   Concorde (flewed   flew) over our town today.

5   Mr Taylor (brought   bought) some plants at the market.

6   Britain's rugby team (winned   won) all their matches in Australia.

C Write this passage, putting all the verbs into the past tense.

Frank is making a new box for his tools. He buys pieces of wood and saws them to the right size. He thinks they are big enough, but he speaks to his father and gets his advice. He tells his father the size, and his father thinks it is just right.

So Frank goes ahead with his plans and builds the box. He then shows it to his father who tells him he can be proud of it.

Present participle

The present participle always ends in **ing**. It is used to make the present continuous tense, to describe an action which is still going on.

Example:

Dave and Sheila are **playing** records.

The past continuous tense is made by putting the auxiliary verb into the past tense.

Example:

It **was** raining when we left home.

Present and past participles can also be used as adjectives.

Examples:

sitting room
polished floor

A   Write the present participle of these verbs.

show   live   buy   swim   enjoy   hold   spell   run   watch   strike   suffer
wear   dance   surprise

B   Write this passage. Put the verbs in orange into the past continuous tense.

The light faded and darkness descended on the valley. One or two lights appeared in the windows of the cottages. The chattering of the birds ceased and silence fell like a blanket over the world around. Only an owl hooted. Nicola listened to the wings of night-birds which flew overhead. She felt a shiver of fear while she ran back to the welcome light and warmth of her house.

C   Write a phrase with an adjective to describe each of these pictures. Each adjective should be a participle made from the verb under the picture.

1   wash   2   laugh   3   close   4   limp

Future tense

The future tense tells us what is going to happen.
It is made by putting the auxiliaries **shall** or **will** before the main verb.
Use **shall** with **I** and **we**.
Use **will** with **you, he, she, it, they** or nouns.

Examples: I shall go shopping   We shall be there.

He will enjoy the holiday.   The train will be here soon.

Note: In speech, the auxiliary is often shortened.

Examples: I shall → I'll   you will → you'll   we shall not → we shan't
he will not → he won't

A   Write these sentences. Put shall or will in the spaces.

1   Our visitors ——— arrive at ten o'clock.

2   We ——— not know which team we play until next week.

3   ——— I stay, or will Trevor be staying?

4   Mum ——— decide tomorrow when we ——— have the party.

B   Write these sentences. Put the future tense of the verb in brackets in the spaces.

1   The train ——— at Woking and Southampton on the way. (stop)

2   I know we ——— a good time. (have)

3   ——— you ——— Ben for a walk? (take)

4   The committee ——— a decision tomorrow. (make)

5   Sara ——— you if you have any problems. (help)

C   Write this passage. Put shall or will (or the shortened form) in the spaces where appropriate

"I ——— be ready soon," said Rex.
"All right," said Gerry. "We ——— be waiting outside."
Four boys ——— be going for a hike across the moors. They ——— catch a
bus from the town and ——— leave the bus after an hour's journey, and then
——— walk to a hill top, where they ——— have a packed lunch.
"You ——— enjoy it," said Gerry, who ——— act as guide.
"We certainly ——— ," said the others.
The hike is a long one and the boys ——— be tired when they get home.

Transitive and intransitive verbs

A transitive verb tells of the action of a subject on an object.

Example:

Ronnie (subject) moved (transitive verb) the chair (object).

An intransitive verb does not need an object to complete the meaning of the sentence.

Example:

Ronnie (subject) sat down (intransitive verb).

The same verb might be intransitive in one sentence, and transitive in another.

Examples:

Patrick **woke** early. (intransitive)
Patrick **woke** his brother early. (transitive)

A The verbs in these sentences are intransitive. Write the sentences again, giving each verb an object to make it transitive.

1 I can hear.

2 Do you see?

3 The batsman hit hard.

4 Roger played for our enjoyment.

B In this passage, five of the verbs in orange are transitive, and five are intransitive. Make a list of each kind of verb.

The train arrived on time, and many passengers poured out. Those waiting on the platform boarded the train. One or two asked the guard the time of arrival at the next station.

Then the guard blew his whistle. The train started. The guard checked his watch, and walked up the corridor to punch tickets.

C Are the verbs in these sentences transitive or intransitive? Make a list of each kind of verb.

1 We sold many articles at the jumble sale.

2 Our team won the match by two goals to nil.

3 Julie cooked her own breakfast as her mother was ill.

4 Can anyone tell me if Wendy is coming?

5 Maureen hesitated, for she felt afraid.

6 Gary said he was going back.

Active and passive verbs

A verb is said to be active when the subject of the sentence does the action.

Examples:

Nasreen **stroked** the cat.
Derek **kicked** the ball.

The verb is said to be passive when the subject of the sentence receives the action.

Examples:

The cat **was stroked** by Nasreen.
The ball **has been kicked** by Derek.
So the verbs **stroke** and **kick** can be used actively or passively.

Note: Not all verbs can be used actively and passively. Only transitive verbs can be used in these ways.

A Write these sentences, changing the verb from active to passive.

Example: The puppy buried the bone. → The bone was buried by the puppy.

1 The golfer hit the ball a long way with his club.

2 Kathryn made some mince pies.

3 The motorist knocked down the old lady.

4 The soldiers attacked the garrison.

5 Mary washed and polished the floor.

6 Before the end of the year the builders built the house.

B This passage is written in the passive voice. Write it again in the active voice.

The garden shed was put up by Tom Brown and his brothers. The site for the shed had been measured and levelled by Tom. The sections of the shed had been prepared by Richard. Then the shed had been erected by Tom and his brothers Richard and Robert.

When the shed had been bolted together by the brothers, it had been painted by Robert. Finally, it had been inspected by father, and the brothers had been praised by him for a splendid piece of work.

Think back

A   Make a list of the verbs in this passage.

The cricket match was between the Casuals and the school Old Boys. The Casuals batted first, and they were expected to win. The spectators remembered how well they had played during the season.

Their opening batsman lammed the first ball to the boundary for a four. He swung his bat round and hit the second ball hard, lobbing it up in the air. A fielder ran forward but missed the catch. Then the batsman steadied himself and grabbed every run he could. The Old Boys' best bowler then bowled a fast one. The batsman tapped it to one side, and started to run. A fieldsman took it, and swept off the bails of the wicket. The umpire signalled 'out'.

B   Write this passage correctly. The past tenses in orange are all incorrect.

Hilary come home from school and begun to help her mother, who was ill. She sweeped the floors, shaked the mats and drawed some water to make a cup of tea. She taked the tea to her mother who had lied down in bed.

After she had drank her own tea, Hilary begun to wash the tea towels. She had wringed out the towels and had threw them on to a radiator to dry. The she feeled tired and laid down to rest.

C   Write the verb from which each of these nouns is made, and write the present participle and simple past tense of each verb.

Example: swimmer → swim   swimming   swam

manager   servant   entrance   baker   building   weaver   drawing   singer speaker   sweeper

D   Hashim wrote this letter to his friend Robin. But he did not speak English very well and made many mistakes. Write the letter again for him correctly.

Dear Robin,

I had meaned to write to you yesterday, but I had wrote to my brother and had forgetted to buy some more paper at the post office. When I sawed you on Monday, I forgetted to tell you that it is my birthday today. I have been gave many presents of toys and I have playing with them all day. I have drawed with my crayons, have sticked stamps in my new album, and have throwed darts at my dart board. I have broke my new bat and have payed to have it mended.

I was pleased to have meeted you on Monday.

Hashim.

E Bakeesh and his sister Bindoo went to the circus. Write a short account of what they saw.

F Copy this crossword and fill in the words from the clues. All the words are verbs.

1		2		3
	▓		▓	
4				
	▓		▓	
5				

Clues

Across:

1 To suppose something without being certain
4 To wake up
5 To throw out

Down:

1 For an animal to eat grass
2 To rub out
3 To perspire

G Make two lists of the verbs in this passage. Head the lists TRANSITIVE VERBS and INTRANSITIVE VERBS.

The Burtons were moving from their old house to a newly-built house which stood on an estate. Donald Burton and his sister Angela were very excited. The carpets had been laid in the new house, mother was waiting for the men to arrive, while father stayed behind at the old house to see that nothing was left.

Donald and Angela were with their mother when the van arrived and the men unloaded the furniture. "When do we have tea?" Angela asked her mother. "Oh, we shall eat something about five o'clock," mother said.

H Complete this story by using the verbs in the box to fill the spaces. Use each verb once only.

are	bought	caught
cooked	fried	grew
laid	lit	pitched
prepared	rose	sat
struck	was	went

Ron and Harold ——— two hikers who ——— camping. They ——— a tent and then Harold ——— a fire. He ——— a match and ——— the fire. Soon there ——— a cheerful blaze. When the fire ——— hot, Ron ——— a meal. He ——— some fish which he ——— in a nearby stream. He ——— it in fat which he ——— from a local shop. The smell of cooking ——— from the pan and soon the boys ——— down to a good meal.

Pronouns

A pronoun is a word that stands in place of a noun.

Example: "Ask Mr Brown if **he** will see me now."

The word **he** is a pronoun standing for the noun Mr Brown.

These words are pronouns.	**he**	**her**	**him**	**I**	**it**	**me**	**she**	**they**
	us	**we**	**what**	**who**	**whoever**	**you**		

A   Make a list of the pronouns in these sentences.

1   The cycle dealer said he would soon repair it.

2   So you think I should buy a present for uncle?

3   Who would like to come with me?

4   They would not believe me when I told them the story.

5   They all heard his suggestion, and they all agreed to it.

6   Whoever told her that I said it has not understood me!

B   Put suitable pronouns in the spaces of this passage.

   Simon met his old friend Jeremy the other day. ——— had not seen ———
for years. ——— had changed during that time, but his voice was the same.
   "Where have ——— been?" ——— asked ——— .
   "Oh, ——— went north to Leeds for five years," Jeremy replied. "My family
had to move there. ——— all enjoyed the change."
   " ——— must come to our house," ——— said, and ——— can tell ——— all
about ——— ."
   "OK," said Jeremy, " ——— shall come tomorrow."
   "Bring your sister along," ——— said. " ——— should like to see ——— and
hear what ——— thought of the change. Give my best wishes to all of ——— at
home!"

C   Write these sentences. Use pronouns to replace the nouns where suitable.

1   Frank took the book off the shelf, then Frank gave the book to his little sister.

2   Maggie said that Maggie felt ill.

3   The doctor told Mrs Reeves that the doctor would see Mrs Reeves next.

4   The team deserved to win the cup because the team had played so well.

Possessive pronouns

A possessive pronoun shows ownership or possession.

Examples: This book is **mine**. It belongs to me.

This book is **yours**. It belongs to you.

These words are   **his   hers   mine   ours   theirs   yours**
possessive pronouns.

A Put a possessive pronoun in each space.

1 These seats are ——— , and those are ——— .

2 Which of these coats is ——— , and which is ——— ?

3 Both cases are heavy, but ——— is heavier than ——— .

4 I am not sure which house is ——— .

5 This is ——— with the initials on.

6 The train on platform two is ——— .

7 That football belongs to Richard. It's ——— .

8 Yvonne shouted, "The sweets are not ——— . They're ——— !"

B Make a list of the possessive pronouns in this passage.

The woodwork class had arranged an exhibition of models they had made at school. The exhibition had been a great success, and now the pupils were sorting out their models to take home.

"This doll's house is mine," said Barry. "I made it for my little sister."

"This trinket box is yours, Terry," said John.

"These skittles are ours," said the Davies twins, "and the stools are theirs," pointing to the Smith brothers.

"Whose is this lampstand?" asked Cedric.

"I think it is his," said Barry, pointing to John. "But his sister helped him, so it is half hers."

The models were soon sorted out and the boys went home, very proud that the exhibition had been theirs.

C Can you make five possessive pronouns out of these letters?

h o e u r y t i s

Adjectives

An adjective is a word which describes a noun.
The adjective may stand next to the noun, or separate from it.

Examples:

He is a tall handsome boy.

The boy was tall and handsome.

Numbers can be used as adjectives.

Examples:

one, two, three, four etc., showing how many.   Two birds flew overhead.

first, second, third, fourth etc., showing position.   Alan was third in the race.

A   Make a list of the adjectives in these sentences.

1   The trapped soldiers were brave and determined.

2   An expert mechanic soon had the old car moving again.

3   Barrie, who was a good footballer, scored three fine goals.

4   There are many fine prizes to be won in the next sports.

5   The setting sun shone with a red glow over the calm sea.

6   The quick brown fox jumped over the lazy dog.

7   Great oaks from little acorns grow.

8   Every cloud has a silver lining.

B   Write a sentence containing two adjectives about each picture.

1   2   3

Possessive adjectives

A possessive adjective shows ownership or possession. It is always placed next to the noun it is describing.

Examples: **My** coat is hanging on a peg.
Where is **its** bone?

her   his   its   my   our   their   your   are possessive adjectives

Note: Do not mix up **its** with **it's**.
its means 'belonging to it'.   **it's** means 'it is'.

A   Put a possessive adjective in each space.

1   Michael showed ——— ticket to the inspector.

2   ——— shoes are in the cupboard, John.

3   The walkers have lost ——— way.

4   The cat lay down in ——— basket.

5   Sara told ——— aunt that she would stay.

6   I have lost ——— purse.

7   We went back to ——— house.

8   We showed ——— certificates to Eirwen and ——— brother.

B   Make a list of the possessive adjectives in this passage.

Our football team has had a good season. They won most of their matches and one, whose result was a draw, should have been won. I told my cousin, who plays for another school, "Your team is second to ours, and when the two teams meet I hope our team keeps its place at the top."
His reply was, "I must tell my sister that. Her forecast is that we shall win."
I hoped that my forecast of our victory would be the right one. In fact their team beat our boys, and took its position at the top of the league.

C   Can you make six possessive adjectives out of these letters?

o   s   h   w   e   i   r   t   u

Formation of adjectives

Many adjectives are formed from verbs or nouns.

1 Some adjectives are formed from verbs.

Examples: annoying (annoy)   startling (startle)   attractive (attract)
dried (dry)   clipped (clip)   bent (bend)   burnt (burn)   woven (weave)

2 Some verbs are used as adjectives.

Examples: press stud   push button   tap dance   lift pump   push cart
skating rink   looking glass   burning glass   rocking chair   revolving door

3 Some adjectives are formed from nouns.

Examples: bony (bone)   marshy (marsh)   golden (gold)   silken (silk)
awful (awe)   dreadful (dread)   musical (music)   merciful (mercy)

4 Some nouns are used as adjectives.

Examples: gold watch   brass band   town hall   village green   football team

A   In this passage seven of the adjectives in orange are formed from nouns, and
seven are formed from verbs. Make lists of each kind.

The fire engine raced down the village street to the boating lake. In the billiards room of the club by the side of the lake a fire had started. Motor boats and sailing boats stopped to see what was happening. The firemen jumped out of their machine, pulled out water hoses, set up a fire escape, and made their way through a revolving door which led into the bar. They used fire extinguishers on the fire, but could not put it out. They attached their hoses to a hydrant in the road, opened a stop cock and the water gushed out. By this time the fire had reached the club's dining room, while a sitting room next door was threatened. Eventually the fire was put out, and the firemen returned along the winding road.

B   Make a list of the names of these six objects, putting two adjectives before each
one. Then from your list write out the adjectives which are formed from nouns.

1   2   3   4   5   6

Comparative adjectives

When we compare two things we add **er** to the adjective.

Example: Jenifer is **taller** than Gwen.

When the adjective is a long one we put **more** in front of it.

Example: This picture is **more beautiful** than that one.

Sometimes the adjective has to be altered before adding **er**.

1   If the adjective ends in **y**, you usually change **y** to **ier**.

sunny → sunnier

2   Very short adjectives often double the last consonant.

fit → fitter   thin → thinner

A   Write these sentences. Make the adjective in orange comparative.

1   The water tank is full than it was yesterday.

2   It is sensible to save some of your money.

3   I think it will rain, as the clouds are grey.

4   Malcolm is trustworthy than the others, and can be relied on.

5   Daisies are common in the fields than cowslips.

6   John is sad than I have seen him for a long time.

7   It is hot today than it was yesterday.

8   You are lucky than I am in guessing games.

B   Write these sentences. Put the correct comparative adjective from the brackets in the space.

1   I feel —— after my holiday. (healthier   more healthy)

2   We found the roads —— at the week-end. (busier   busyer)

3   Debbie's puppy is —— than mine. (tinier   more tiny)

4   Your lawn is —— than ours. (greener   more green)

5   These roses are —— in colour than the others. (oranger   more orange)

6   It is —— to go by this path. (easier   more easy)

7   It is —— to go by this path. (easier   more easy)

Superlative adjectives

> When we compare three or more things we add **est** to the adjective.
>
> **Example:** Jenifer is the **tallest** girl of the three.
>
> When the adjective is a long one we put **most** in front of it.
>
> **Example:** This picture is the **most beautiful** of all.
>
> Sometimes the adjective ending has to be altered before adding **est**.
> The rules for this are the same as for comparative adjectives.

A Write these sentences. Put the correct superlative adjective from the brackets in the space.

1 He is the ———— rower in the boat. (heaviest   most heavy)

2 That was the ————thing to do! (foolishest   most foolish)

3 This glass is the ———— of the sheets. (thinnest   most thin)

4 The inspector said he was the ————criminal he knew. (cunningest   most cunning)

5 Can I have the ———— cabbage you have? (biggest   most big)

6 Roger is the ————member of the team. (reliablest   most reliable)

7 The thief is the ————rogue in town. (slyest   most sly)

B Write these sentences. Make the adjective in orange superlative.

1 This snake is the deadly in the world.

2 Anne is the excitable of girls.

3 Geoff ran the fast race of his career.

4 Climbing the mountain was dangerous near the summit.

5 Olwen's work is the tidy of all.

6 It is the funny story I have heard in years!

7 The Roman Empire was the mighty of the ancient world.

Irregular comparison

Some adjectives have a comparative and a superlative form in which new words are used.

Examples:	**adjective**	**comparative**	**superlative**
	bad	worse	worst
	good	better	best
	little	less	least
	some, many much	more	most

Some adjectives have no comparative or superlative forms.
A thing cannot be more dead, more single, more first, more daily, more fifty, more golden or more perfect.

A Write these sentences filling in the two blanks with the comparative and superlative of the adjective in orange.

1 Tom wanted only a little supper. Diane wanted ———, while Tom wanted ——— of all.

2 Mark had a bad end-of-term report. Sally's report was ———, while Marion's was the ———.

3 I picked some blackberries. Mother picked ———, while father picked the ———.

4 Maureen is a good tennis player. Owen is ———, but Jim is the ———.

B Write what these are.

1 The superlative of merry

2 The comparative of curly

3 The comparative of good

4 The superlative of second

5 The comparative of early

6 The superlative of much

7 The comparative of bad

8 The superlative of comfortable

9 The comparative of little

10 The superlative of single

Adverbs

An adverb is a word which tells us more about a verb. It tells us how, when or where an action of the verb takes place.
An adverb can be formed in three ways.

1   By adding **ly** to an adjective.

Example: Simon rode **slowly** down the road.

2   Some adjectives are used as adverbs, without being changed.

Example: It was raining **hard**.

3   Some words exist only as adverbs.

Example: Ali is **always** working.

An adverb can be used to tell us more about an adjective.

Example: a **beautifully** green garden

A   Write these sentences. Fill each space with an adverb made from the adjective in brackets.

1   Jenny paints ———. (beautiful)

2   Can you see the tower on the hill ———? (plain)

3   Denis slumped ——— in a chair after his long walk. (heavy)

4   "Go back!" he shouted ———. (angry)

5   He was ——— sorry to be late. (awful)

B   Write five sentences, each containing one of these words as an adverb.

once   anyhow   never   sometimes   sideways

C   Write the adverbs, and the verbs they are describing, in these sentences.

1   The thieves crept stealthily from the house.

2   You have done that well.

3   Ballerinas dance gracefully.

4   The belt of rain will move slowly across the country.

5   The bus stopped suddenly and nearly caused an accident.

Comparison of adverbs

Many adverbs have a comparative and superlative form, just like adjectives.

The comparative and superlative of adverbs ending in **ly** are formed by putting **more** and **most** before the adverb.

Example:

slowly   more slowly   most slowly

Add **er** and **est** to other adverbs.

Example:

hard   harder   hardest

Note these two irregular adverbs:

well   better   best

badly   worse   worst

Some adverbs have no comparison.

Examples:

once   always   never   sometimes

Some adverbs are used to describe other adverbs.

Examples:

very   quite   rather   less

A   Write the comparative and superlative forms of these adverbs.

sensibly   truthfully   anywhere   straight   short   never

somehow   well   quickly   twice   gratefully   easily

B   Write these sentences, choosing the correct comparative adverb from the brackets.

1   I can see (more clearly   clearer) when I wear my glasses.

2   We went to my cousin's (more often   oftener) than before.

3   Harold played (more badly   worse) as the game went on.

4   The policeman spoke (more kindly   kindlier) to the little boy than to the burglar.

5   Fiona laughed (more loudly   loudlier) at every joke.

6   A bicycle goes (more smoothly   smoother) when it has been oiled.

7   When I have taken my medicine I feel (more well   better)

8   The balloon rose (more high   higher) after some weight was thrown out.

9   They had to walk (slower   more slowly) as the wind grew stronger.

10   The toboggan travelled (faster   more fast) as it got near the bottom.

Think back

A There are three kinds of adjectives in this passage, all printed in orange. Write them in three lists, headed COMMON ADJECTIVES PROPER ADJECTIVES and POSSESSIVE ADJECTIVES

John Keen, a prosperous business man, was waiting for the London train. He looked at his watch. "It is twenty minutes to three," he told himself. "The train will be here any minute now."

The express train pulled up at the platform, and John Keen entered a first-class compartment. He lay back on the cushioned seat and was soon asleep. He wakened with a sudden start just as the train drew up at Waterloo station. There he was met by his close friend Tom Hardy, another business man, who owned the Eastern Trading Company. The two companions walked together to a famous London restaurant where they ate a hearty meal. Then they went to their club to discuss an important trading deal.

B From what verbs are these adjectives formed?

fried   burnt   admirable   frightening   bent

split   knitted   written   attractive   dried

C From what nouns are these adjectives formed?

comfortable   musical   merciful   awful   silken

courageous   hilly   dreadful   bony   icy

D Write these sentences, putting the comparative of the adjective in brackets in the space.

1 "I am _____ than you," said John. (tall)

2 "My leg feels _____ than when I first knocked it," said Robert. (bad)

3 "This book is far _____ than I expected," said Mavis. (interesting)

4 The ground is _____ than it was this morning. (dry)

5 Your garden looks _____ than I have ever seen it. (good)

6 Mother wears _____ clothes than grandma. (fashionable)

E Make two lists of the words in orange headed POSSESSIVE PRONOUNS and POSSESSIVE ADJECTIVES

An elderly man was walking down the road. He stopped and pulled out a letter from his pocket and read the address on its envelope. A boy ran up to him.

"Is this yours?" he asked, showing him a pound note. "You dropped it when you drew the letter from your pocket."

"Yes," said the old gentleman. "It is mine. My hand must have touched it when I pulled out the letter. Thank you for returning it."

"I am looking for my sister's house," he continued. "Her address is on the envelope. The name is Robinson. Is that the house?" and he pointed.

"No. I don't know whose house that is," said the boy. "But I do know Robinson's. Theirs is a bit further on, next door to ours. We have been their neighbours for years. I'll show you."

F Make adverbs from these adjectives.

slow   painless   hurried   merry   good   loyal   proud   easy   sudden   sensible

G Match each adverb in the orange box with the most suitable verb in the black box.

bravely	gently
happily	comfortably
fast	gratefully
peacefully	hopefully
angrily	equally

accept	shout
sleep	settle
laugh	run
share	stroke
fight	ask

H Write these sentences. Make the adjective or adverb in orange comparative or superlative.

1 Which of these two do you think is clear?

2 Mike is the short-sighted person I have ever met.

3 The first day of our week's holiday was perfect.

4 We must try hard tomorrow than we did today.

5 Jacky swims well than anyone else in the class.

6 It will be cheap to go by train.

7 That was the happy day of my life.

8 Brian will probably wait patiently than Pete.

Conjunctions

A conjunction is a joining word. It joins together two words, phrases or sentences.

Examples: Lena **and** Pauline went to the cinema.

We can't go **until** I've found my purse.

Here are the most common conjunctions:

and but or if until although because so unless as before after when where while

A Write these sentences. Underline the conjunction in each one.

1 The butcher could not deliver the meat as his van had broken down.

2 I will do the shopping if you will give me some money.

3 We will go for a picnic although the weather is doubtful.

4 Kathryn said she would not go unless Jean went too.

5 Julie lost her money so she had to walk home.

6 You can't plant the bulbs until you have prepared the soil.

7 Mark is a good player, but he has his bad days.

8 We went to buy some groceries before the shops closed.

B Write these sentences. Fill each space with a conjunction.

1 Shall we go out ——— it is fine?

2 Marion asked about the art class ——— she decided to join.

3 Clive wanted to learn to swim ——— he needed someone to teach him.

4 Selina passed her examinations ——— she had been ill beforehand.

5 Chris was sad ——— the holiday was over.

6 Will you come and see me ——— you get back from holiday.

7 You had better finish that ——— you go out.

8 ——— they win the match next week, they will be relegated.

9 We will have to choose one ——— the other.

10 Jim lost his wallet ——— he went to the police station.

Sentences

A sentence is a group of words which is complete in itself. It always has a verb. A sentence begins with a capital letter and ends with a full-stop, exclamation mark, or question mark.

Examples: The bird flew over the house.

Did the bird fly over the house?

That batsman hit a 6 out of the ground!

A Which of these are sentences and which are not? Write the sentences and give them the correct punctuation.

1 Jill ran after the cat

2 What shall we do

3 tomorrow's football match

4 look at the rabbit

5 near the shop in the village

6 what a fuss

7 we bought ice-creams

8 ice-creams for sale

B Tom wrote to his friend Dick while on holiday. Unfortunately, he did not write in sentences. Write this part of the letter again, dividing it into sentences and using correct punctuation.

I followed the path until I was out of the wood where do I go now I asked myself then I saw a gate across another path over a meadow I climbed over the locked gate and followed the path soon I came to a road which I recognised this led me back home

C Sentences flow in a certain order. Can you write out these mixed-up sentences so that they make sense?

1 flew tree black over the crow A

2 Britain most is fishing popular sport the in

3 night out cinema we last to the went

4 at long bus queue there was a stop the

Subject and object

Most sentences have a subject and an object, as well as a verb.

Example:

Sheila knitted a **scarf**.

The subject (Sheila) tells you who or what is doing the action in the sentence.
The object (scarf) tells you who or what is receiving the action.

A   Write the subject and the object in these sentences.

1   Tony left work early.

2   We had a lovely holiday.

3   All the boys enjoyed the game.

4   Two men repaired the wall.

5   The wind blew down the wall.

6   Will you please return our ball?

7   Did you like the concert?

8   Alan broke the window.

B   Write these sentences, putting a subject and an object in the spaces.

1   ——— wanted to see the ———.

2   Can ——— play ———?

3   How does ——— like his new ———?

4   The ——— blew the ——— down.

5   My pet ——— ate his ———.

6   Three ——— ran across the ———.

7   ——— wanted to eat some ———.

8   ——— went for a ride on her ———.

C   Write a simple sentence about each picture. Make the part of the picture labelled
S the subject and the part labelled O the object.

Subject and verb agreement

The subject of a sentence and its verb must agree. If the subject is singular, the verb must be singular too.

Examples:

The bottle **is** empty.

The bottles **are** empty.

Some words always take singular verbs.

These are:
Collective nouns.
Money, length, weights and time.
Words like everybody, anybody, nobody, each, either, either . . . or, neither . . . nor.

A Write these sentences, choosing the correct verb from the brackets.

1 The overalls (is   are) too big for me.

2 Every one of the boys (has   have) done his homework.

3 You (was   were) both seen at the pictures last night.

4 Which (is   are) cheaper, ham and eggs or bacon and beans?

5 The crowd (pour   pours) out of the ground.

6 (Has   Have) the bats and balls been cleared away?

7 Either Sam or Martin (is   are) to blame.

8 The town council (meet   meets) this afternoon.

9 The number of foreign cars (is   are) growing.

10 Everybody who (want   wants) to come will be welcome.

11 They (was   were) thrilled to meet their hero.

12 You (was   were) late home yesterday.

B There are many mistakes in this passage, because subject and verb do not always agree. Write the passage out correctly.

The school governing board have decided that the team can use the school field in the holidays. The captain and his players wants to use it two mornings a week. Every one of the players are keen to practise, but neither of the two full-backs are playing their best at present. The crowd were very pleased with the team at their last match and it were a real pleasure to see the team in top form.

Clauses and compound sentences

A sentence which has only one verb is called a simple sentence. If two sentences are joined together by the conjunctions **and**, **but** or **or** it is called a compound sentence.

The two original sentences are then called clauses of the new sentence. Each clause is of equal importance and is called a main clause.

Example:

We missed the train but we were still on time.

　　　main clause　　　　　　main clause

A　Join these pairs of sentences using and, but or or.

1　Sarah fed her cat well. The cat became ill.

2　Colin borrowed his brother's bike. He cycled to the shops.

3　I read this book about climbers. The book was boring.

4　We can cross the channel by hovercraft. We can fly across.

5　Sue likes the watch very much. It is rather expensive.

6　Rachel was lost in the wood. Rachel became frightened.

7　You had better clear up now. You will get into trouble.

8　Ted tried to jump over the wall. He fell and hurt himself.

9　The sun shone. Our sports' day was a big success.

10　He switched the television off. He went to bed.

B　Write a compound sentence to describe each of these pictures.

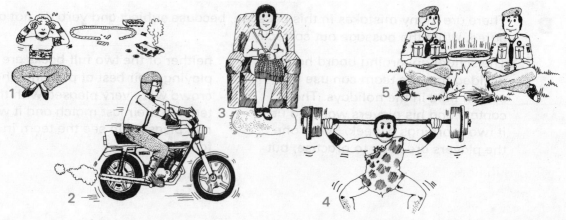

Clauses and complex sentences

Simple sentences joined together by conjunctions other than **and, but** or **or** make a complex sentence. The clauses in a complex sentence are not of equal importance. There is a main clause and one (or more) subordinate clause. The subordinate clause depends on the main clause to complete its meaning.

Example:

We enjoyed ourselves even though it rained.
└── **main clause** ──┘ └**subordinate clause**┘

even though is the conjunction.

A Using conjunctions from the box, join these clauses to make complete sentences.

where	which	wherever	because	who
as	so	although	before	while	until

1 The captain decided not to leave port ——— the steering was faulty ——— it could not be relied on.

2 • We picked blackberries ——— we could find them ——— we had as many as we wanted.

3 Catherine asked her father for some money ——— she wanted to buy some gloves ——— the sale was over.

4 ——— he lost the Battle of Waterloo, Napoleon was a great leader, ——— the French like to remember him.

B Write out the subordinate clauses in this passage adapted from Captain Marryat's 'The Children of the New Forest'.

Edward, who had by this time got over half his journey, looked up. He was confronted by a powerful man, who was about forty years of age, and who was dressed as a verderer of the forest.

"How now, young fellow. What are you doing here?" said the man, who walked up to him and cocked the gun he held in his hand. Edward quietly cocked his own gun, which was loaded.

"I am walking across the forest, as you can see," he said.

"Yes, I can see that, but you are walking with a dog and a gun. Deer stalkers are no longer permitted to range this forest, so you will be pleased to walk with me."

Adverb clauses

An adverb clause tells you more about the verb in the main clause. It may tell you:

1   when, where or for how long something happens, with these conjunctions.
    when   before   after   until   as   while   as soon as

2   how or why something happens, with these conjunctions.
    because   as   since   for   so   so that   in order that   as if

3   what can or must happen before something else follows, with these conjunctions.
    if   unless   although   even if

Examples:

Father paid the man **when he had finished the work**. (time)

John searched for his wallet **where he had lost it**. (place)

Tim went swimming **because he enjoyed it**. (reason why)

A   Complete the adverb clause after the conjunction in these sentences.

1   I came home when ———.

2   Sheila did not buy a dress although ———.

3   The referee blew his whistle because ———.

4   If ———, the girls will go for a walk.

5   As soon as ———, the lifeboats raced to the sinking ship.

6   Unless ———, I cannot paint the fence.

7   We will wait here until ———.

8   They only just had time to move out of the way before ———.

9   Look before ———.

10 Mark's mother gave him some money so that ———.

B   Uandra and Lena are having a conversation. They are talking about school. Write three or four sentences about their conversation. In each sentence include an adverb clause. Make sure you join the adverb clause to the main clause of the sentence with a conjunction.

C   Write three adverb clauses from this passage.

Trevor Keen, sergeant in the police detective force, was sitting in his office writing reports, when the telephone rang. As soon as he heard the telephone message, he sprang to his feet.

He had been told that a neighbour, while he was gardening, saw a man enter the house next door.

Sergeant Keen sped away in a police car, while a constable took charge of the police station. He was just in time to prevent a burglary, although he finished his day at a very late hour.

D   Write three adverb clauses from this passage.

Mr Smith, the manager of a well-known firm, decided to take a holiday as soon as the school holidays began. Alec and Debbie, his two children at a boarding school, were coming home for their holidays in a week's time. The whole family was going to Spain because they liked the sunshine. The children also looked forward to bathing in the warm sea, although neither of them could swim well. The organisation making all their arrangements had reserved their accommodation. Even though they had not yet received their travel tickets, Mr Smith felt sure they would have a good holiday.

E   Write the sentences which contain an adverb clause.

1   Mother went shopping, while Colin went out to play.

2   The manager of the firm, a man of great experience, was efficient.

3   They abandoned the idea of a walk, since it was raining hard.

4   We did not believe those who told us the story.

5   Whichever tennis racket you choose you can keep.

6   Andrew walked home, whistling all the way.

7   As soon as I had finished reading the story, I went to bed.

8   Mrs Johnson decided to go out even though she had a headache.

Adjective clauses

An adjective clause tells you more about the noun or pronoun in the main clause. It is joined to the main clause by a pronoun – called the relative pronoun.

who, which, that, whose and **whom** are relative pronouns.

Examples:

The cap **that I found** is here.

The boy **who helped the old lady** has gone home.

That is the man **whose car broke down**.

A   Write the adjective clause in each of these sentences.

1   We are playing against a team which has not lost a match.

2   The man who was wanted by the police stepped out of the train.

3   I am returning the book that you lent me.

4   I will show you the boy whose dog is lost.

5   Mary has a hamster that will not eat its food.

B   Write an adjective clause in each of these sentences, choosing the right relative pronoun from the brackets.

1   The horse (who   which) galloped away has been found.

2   The cat (who   that) I keep has been ill.

3   My uncle has a house (whose   that) garden is full of plants.

4   The boys (which   who) were wet have dried their clothes.

C   Put the letters under each picture in the right order, to make an adjective describing the picture. Then write a sentence, with an adjective clause containing the adjective.

Example: The bag, which is made of leather, will be useful.

elhetra   vyelil   nignhsi   drite   mosouren

Noun clauses

A noun clause is a clause with its own subject and verb, which stands for a noun. Like a noun, it can be either the subject or the object of a sentence.

Examples:

Whoever is chosen as captain must attend the meetings.

She felt sure **that they would come.** (that is, **of their coming**)

Why he played so badly is a puzzle to me. (that is, **his bad play**)

A Write the noun clauses in these sentences.

1 The girl chosen as head prefect was good at both schoolwork and sport.

2 What they will do next remains to be seen.

3 Whatever rules are made must be obeyed.

4 Where I should put these books is a problem.

5 I am not clear about what is going to happen.

6 Can you tell me what the time is?

7 They were told that the game was cancelled.

8 Those going to camp are on the train.

B Complete these sentences by adding suitable noun clauses.

1 The angry farmer told me ———.

2 ——— we must obey them.

3 We cannot disagree with ———.

4 He will help you with ———.

5 The deaf woman could not understand ———.

C How many noun clauses can you find in this passage? Write them out.

Beryl's friend Sue was ill in bed. How she became ill was a mystery.

"Sue is always so fit," Beryl said to the others. "I don't understand what she has caught. But whatever illness it is has made her feel bad."

Sue was one of those chosen to play in the hockey team. Beryl was afraid Sue could not play next week. Those in the team had to practise regularly. She was not sure whether Sue would be fit for the game.

Luckily, Sue was soon well and was able to join the others for the first match.

49

Think back

A Add some more words to make these into sentences.

1 what fun!

2 after she had come home

3 ten small cakes

4 near where we live

5 just as we reached the park

6 three of the pups

B Write these sentences, putting a subject and an object in the spaces.

1 —— wanted to see the ——.

2 Can —— play ——?

3 How does —— like his new ——?

4 The —— blew the —— down.

5 My pet —— ate his ——.

6 Three —— crossed the ——.

7 —— wanted to buy some ——.

8 —— went for a ——.

C Write this passage correctly, making the subjects and verbs agree.

My friend Atma and I wants to have a day out together. So we goes to the park to feed the ducks. The town council have made a new rule that the park opens later in winter. So when we gets there the gates is closed. But we climbs over. It were a foolish thing to do, and I tears my trousers. After playing for an hour we feels hungry. So we goes to a café for something to eat.

D Write this passage. Choose a conjunction to introduce each adverb clause.

I do not like cycling through the town —— the traffic is so heavy. It is not easy to keep a steady course —— cars and lorries are whizzing past. I feel relieved —— I reach quieter roads. I have to use my bicycle —— I am attending the Technical College. I shall be leaving soon, —— I shall probably find work in the town. Unfortunately I should then have to use my bicycle again, —— I am not on a bus route.

E Put who, whom or whose in the space in each sentence.

1 To —— shall I give the prize?

2 The girl in the yellow dress is the one —— sang best.

3 —— coat is this?

4 Is that the lady about —— you were talking?

5 —— can tell me where Newbury Road is?

F   Write the adjective clauses in this passage.

Wilma was having a holiday with one of her friends, whose father was a farmer. One day she rode down the lane on a pony, which the farmer had lent her. She met two men, one of whom looked like a foreigner. He asked her the way to the farm, which she had just left. The pony, which was very restive, moved away. She called to the man, for whom she had stopped, that the farm was down the lane.

G   Choose suitable words from the box to complete these complex sentences.

| until | although | as | because |
| since | before | and | who | when |

1   John always wants to go fishing ——— he has a day's holiday.

2   They stayed inside ——— the rain stopped ——— they did not want to get wet.

3   Laura ran to her friend's house ——— she wanted to see her ——— she went out.

4   Owen could not get to school in time ——— his bicycle tyre was punctured ——— it would take him a long time to repair.

5   The children, ——— like the seaside, always look forward to their holiday, ——— neither of them can swim well.

H   Describe this scene in six sentences.

Punctuation

Punctuation is a matter of putting in a sentence a full stop, question mark, exclamation mark, comma, colon, hyphen, speech marks or quotation marks.

- A full stop is placed at the end of a sentence. Every sentence begins with a capital letter, and ends with a full stop, a question mark or an exclamation mark.

? A question mark takes the place of a full stop when a question is asked.

! An exclamation mark is used to express anger or excitement.

, A comma marks a short pause in a sentence. It is used to separate items on a list, or several adjectives, or a phrase within a sentence.

A Write these sentences. Use one of the punctuation marks shown above to take the place of each ★

1 Where are you going on holiday this year★

2 Henry VIII★ who lived at Hampton Court★ had six wives★

3 I could hardly believe my eyes★

4 The black★ silky coat of the dog gleamed in the sunlight★

5 Did you know that Peter★ who used to live next door★ has moved to

Aberdeen★

B Write this passage, putting in capital letters and punctuation marks where needed.

julia and her cousin wendy were on holiday in southpool the first morning after they arrived they walked to the sandy shore intending to have a swim but when they came to the shore a very high tide was in and they had to change their plans

instead they went to the fun fair where they spent a long time on the big dipper then they bought some ice-creams before going for a walk on the pier

: A colon may be used to mark the beginning of a list or before direct speech.

" . . . " Speech marks are placed at the beginning and end of words actually spoken by someone.

' . . . ' Quotation marks are placed at the beginning and end of the title of a film, book or play, or a quotation.

— A hyphen is used to join two words often put together and to show where a word has been broken between two lines.

A Write these sentences, putting in capital letters where needed. Use a punctuation mark to take the place of each★.

1 ★i know where my purse is★★ said jean★ ★i left it in the shop★★

2 ★do you see that bird★★ said peter★ ★it is a pied wagtail★★

3 ★i am going to the cinema to see the adventures of sherlock holmes★★ said gwen★★ ★would you like to come with me★★

4 ★hurry up★★ said jeff★ ★or we shall be late for the train★★

5 ★here are the ingredients for the cake★★ said mother★ ★write them down★ flour butter raisins baking powder milk★★

6 ★remember the proverb★★ said father★ ★★a stitch in time saves nine★ ★★

B Write this passage, putting in punctuation marks where needed.

Tricia and her mother were about to go to the market We want potatoes carrots onions and cabbage said Mother May we have beetroot too asked Tricia I do like beetroot Yes said Mother I shall get some if I see some good ones Mother wrote down a list of all the things she wanted Vegetables potatoes carrots onions cabbage beetroot Groceries flour sugar lard butter tea coffee We dont need them all now said Mother But I will get them now while I have time to go and while they are in good supply After all a bird in the hand is worth two in the bush

Prepositions

A preposition is a word which shows the relationship between two nouns or pronouns.

Examples: The book lies **on** the table.

The cat is **under** the bed.

Here are some common prepositions.

about around between inside outside under above at beyond into

over across before by near past up after behind down of

round against below during off through with beneath from on

to among beside in opposite towards

A Write a sentence containing each of these prepositions.

upon below during before against by through across

B Make a list of the prepositions in this passage.

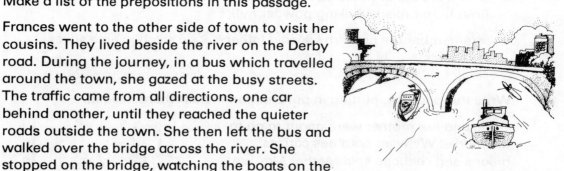

Frances went to the other side of town to visit her cousins. They lived beside the river on the Derby road. During the journey, in a bus which travelled around the town, she gazed at the busy streets. The traffic came from all directions, one car behind another, until they reached the quieter roads outside the town. She then left the bus and walked over the bridge across the river. She stopped on the bridge, watching the boats on the river below.

C Write these sentences. Fill each space with a preposition.

1 I got off the bus ——— the nearest stop.

2 We rowed ——— the river until our arms ached.

3 "Put that back ——— the cupboard!" he shouted.

4 The orange was divided ——— the four friends.

5 The window cleaner leant his ladder ——— the wall of the house.

It is important to use the right preposition with the words before it and after it.

Example: Janice agreed **with** her mother **to** wash up after breakfast.

(We agree **with** someone, but we agree **to** do something.)

Here are other examples showing which preposition to use with a verb or adjective going before it.

accuse of

angry with

annoyed with

blame for

complain to (a person)

complain about (something)

different from

disappointed with

filled with

full of

good for

guilty of

offended with (a person)

offended at (something)

opposite to

part with (a thing)

part from (a person)

rely on

similar to

suffer from

A   Write these sentences, choosing the correct word from the brackets.

1   Our friends walked ———— us in the High Street. (past   passed)

2   We move ———— our new house tomorrow. (into   in)

3   Tracey went to see Mary in hospital and stood ———— her bed.
(besides   beside)

4   Mr Brown was disappointed ———— his son's examination results. (at   with)

5   She was accused ———— cheating. (of   with)

6   The film was different ———— what I expected. (from   to)

7   Father was ashamed ———— what Jimmy had done. (with   of   at)

8   We were all annoyed ———— Valerie and her tricks. (at   with)

B   Rewrite the passage, putting in the right prepositions instead of the words in orange.

Jack stood besides his brother waiting to go in the cinema.

"It is half passed two," he said. "I'm disappointed at them for not opening the doors. I feel like complaining with someone about it."

"Never mind!" said brother Vincent. "I don't feel annoyed with it. We shall soon be inside. Beside, I don't want to go in yet, until Bob comes. I have some sweets to share between the three of us."

Phrases

A phrase is a group of words which contains no verb. Because it contains no verb it is neither a clause nor a sentence. A phrase is often introduced by a preposition.

Examples:

a group of trees

by the pond

A Join these pairs of phrases with a verb to make them into sentences.

1 The great brown bear ——— behind the bars of the cage.

2 Five large rabbits ——— across the meadow.

3 His birthday party ——— a very happy one for Peter.

4 The group ——— their latest hit record.

5 What a large aeroplane ——— on the runway.

6 A raging torrent ——— down the hillside.

B Five of these are sentences and five are phrases. Write the phrases, adding a verb and any other words to make them into sentences.

1 Jill ran after the black cat.

2 Such a fuss!

3 What shall we do when we go to the beach?

4 Simon thanked his uncle.

5 Because of the cold weather.

6 After the school concert.

7 Are you sure what he said is true?

8 Look, there goes a buzzard!

9 Three large white swans.

10 Near the village green.

C Jill and Joan are talking together, sometimes in sentences and sometimes in phrases. Which are the phrases?

"I went to the circus yesterday," said Jill to Joan.
"Lucky you!"
"There were clowns," said Jill.
"How many?"
"Oh, at least three."
"What fun!"

Direct speech

Direct speech is the reporting of words exactly as they are spoken. Direct speech should begin and end with inverted commas (speech marks) **" "**.

Examples: "Can you tell me if Mr Brown lives here?" the stranger asked.

"Can you tell me," the stranger asked, "where Mr Brown lives?"

The inverted commas finish after the comma, full stop or other punctuation mark at the end of the spoken words.

Direct speech is used a great deal in story-writing to make the characters more real. When two people are talking to each other, the words of each speaker start a new paragraph. This helps us to see at a glance who is talking.

A   Write these sentences, putting speech marks round the words that are in direct speech.

1   Arthur exclaimed, We have forgotten our tickets!

2   What a lovely show, said Samantha. I am enjoying it.

3   What is that bird called? whispered Trixie. Can you tell me?

4   How many weeks is it from the party? asked Ralph. Is it five or six? he went on doubtfully. I can't be sure.

5   The speaker addressed the meeting: We have gathered here to do honour to our chairman. He coughed, and then continued. He has served us well for twenty years.

B   Write this conversation between two friends, putting in speech marks where necessary and starting the words of each speaker on a new line.

I like tennis, said Marjorie. Don't you? No, said Karen. I am not very good at it. You must practise more, said Marjorie. You will soon improve. Are you a member of a club? asked Karen. No, I play in the park. Are there tennis courts in the park? Yes, both grass and hard courts. Which do you like playing on most? The grass courts, said Marjorie.

Indirect speech

Indirect speech is used to report what is said without using the actual words spoken. Inverted commas are not used for indirect speech.

Example: The stranger asked if I could tell him whether Mr Brown lived here.

The pronouns in direct speech may be altered when changing to indirect speech.

Example: "**I** should like to know **your** name," he said. (direct)
He said **he** would like to know **my** name. (indirect)

Indirect speech is used especially in newspaper reporting. In reporting a speech, the actual words are not important. What is important is to report what the speaker has to say in as few words as possible. Here indirect speech is best.

A   Write these sentences in indirect speech.

1   "What a lovely day it is," said Gwen.

2   "Barrie," said mother, "have you got your keys?"

3   "Look out!" shouted Bruce. "Mind that barbed wire."

4   "It is fifty miles away," said the driver. "We shan't be there on time."

5   "The grocer's is closed," said Pam. "I can't buy the flour."

B   Write these sentences in direct speech.

1   Linda asked David to pass her the book.

2   Mr Rogers exclaimed that he had forgotten it was his birthday.

3   The woman complained to the greengrocer that he had sold her some bad apples.

4   Tania said she was tired and would have to go home.

5   David told Uncle Simon that he liked his present very much.

C   Give a short account, in indirect speech, of the chairman's speech at the annual meeting of a football or hockey club. Describe the success of the teams and whether there had been any changes in membership.

Word shortening

Contractions

Sometimes, when we are speaking, we run two words into one. This is called a contraction.

An apostrophe is used to show that one or more letters are missing.

Examples:

"**I'm** going for a walk." (**I am**)

"**It's** getting late." (**It is**)

"They **won't** be able to go." (**will not**)

"**You'll** lose that if **you're** not careful." (**you will**   **you are**)

A The words in orange in this passage are contractions. Write out the passage with all the words written in full.

"Here's a queer thing," said Trevor.

"What's the matter?" asked Owen.

"There's a dead mouse on the ground, and I can't understand how it died," answered Trevor. "It doesn't seem to have been killed by another animal, for its body is unmarked, although I'm not sure."

"Well," said Owen, "I shouldn't be surprised if a bird dropped it. It's lying on a stone, and it mightn't be dead."

At that moment the mouse stirred, and then ran away.

"All's well!', exclaimed Trevor. "Who'd have thought it would recover so quickly? Poor thing, I hope it'll be all right."

B Make a list of the numbers 1 to 7. Opposite each number write one word made by shortening the two words in orange in each sentence.

1 Pat might not be able to play in the match.

2 Who is that lady?

3 Maureen and Karen will not be able to go.

4 Eric and Sam have not decided yet.

5 Who will be refereeing the game?

6 "No," said Charles, "I shall not be there."

7 Tim said he would not be joining us.

Making long words shorter

We shorten many long words, so that we can speak more quickly and easily.

Examples:

mum (mother)	cycle (bicycle)	photo (photograph)
dad (father)	phone (telephone)	Pam (Pamela)
Tim (Timothy)	mac (mackintosh)	bus (omnibus)

A Write this passage, putting shorter words in place of those in orange.

Lillian and her brother Reginald bicycled to the house of their aunt Patricia, where they were to stay for tea. They had telephoned their aunt saying they would arrive about three o'clock.

But as they rode quickly along the smooth tar-macadam road, meeting an occasional motorcar, they arrived early. They found their grandmother wheeling a perambulator round the garden. She was wearing a mackintosh as it had started to rain. Their cousin Frederick arrived soon afterwards on his new motorbicycle.

"Let me take your photographs," he called, taking out a camera.

Then they went inside, and there were strawberries and cream for tea, from the refrigerator, followed by cakes.

B Write the shorter names of the objects shown below.

Abbreviations

An abbreviation is a short form used in writing.

Example: Street → St

A full stop is put at the end of the word to show it has been abbreviated, unless the last letter of the word is used to finish the abbreviation. Weights and measures are often abbreviated without a full stop.

Examples: captain → capt.

department → dept

gram → g

Initials are often used as abbreviations. They can be written with or without full stops.

Examples: headquarters → H.Q.
I owe you → IOU

You will find a list of common abbreviations on pages 93 and 94.

A Match the short forms in the orange box with the full words in the black box.

Rev.	U.S.A.	Bros
etc.	Sgt	S.S.
A.A.	Prof.	B.B.C.
Snr	ml.	pm
oz.	B.C.	

Brothers   Senior   millilitre   Sailing Ship

etcetera   Reverend   ounce   Professor

British Broadcasting Corporation

Sergeant   United States of America

post meridiem (afternoon)

Automobile Association   Before Christ

B Write the full form of these abbreviations.

R.N.   Y.H.A.   Feb.   B.R.   kg.   P.O.   O.H.M.S.   m.p.h.

P.T.O.   Co-op.   l.b.w.   masc.   N.H.S.   Nov.   R.A.F.   V.C.

C The abbreviations in the box are all parts of speech. They are often used in dictionaries. List the words below in alphabetical order and use the abbreviations to say what part of speech each one is.

v.   n.   prep.   adv.   adj.   conj.

steal   to   apple   blue   and   slowly
under   slow   joint   bite   although

Think back

A Write this passage, putting in all the capital letters and missing punctuation.

have you heard of this unusual house in north devon no one is sure of its history but the story goes that there lived in the village a man who spent all his time gambling apparently his luck was so good that he made a fortune and as a permanent reminder of his good luck he had a house built which looked as though it was made of playing cards to carry the idea further the house was made with fifty two windows representing the number of cards in a pack its certainly an odd story.

B Write these sentences, putting in capital letters where needed. Use a punctuation mark to take the place of each ★.

1 this is what you will need★ flour★ eggs★ butter and milk★

2 ★where on earth have you been★★ exclaimed linda★ as chris arrived an hour late★

3 ★have you met your future brother★in★law yet★★ asked karen★

4 ★i★m afraid i can★t go any faster★★ said the taxi driver★

5 the boys★ father arranged to meet them at four o★clock★

C Re-arrange the letters in these words to make prepositions.

raw dots   on it   rove   ben hid   dun oar   lilt

D Write these sentences, choosing the correct preposition from the brackets.

1 I have more money ——— this. (beside   besides)

2 Sam dived ——— the water. (in   into)

3 This is different ——— what I expected. (from   to)

4 They waited until the room was full ——— people. (with   of)

5 Share this ——— the two of you. (between   among)

6 The supporters were disappointed ——— the result. (at   with)

E   Match the phrases from the two orange boxes and join them with a verb from the black box to make six complete and sensible sentences.

The cunning fox	is played	hockey for her school.
"What a lovely prize!"	replied	the largest chicken.
The annual cricket match	has played	the confused suspect.
The Tower of London	exclaimed	on the village green.
Sally	stole	famous all over the world.
"I don't know,"	is	the lucky winner.

F   Write these sentences in direct speech.

1   Clare said she would meet Chris the next day.

2   The headmaster announced that term would end on 19 July.

3   Father said he was sorry that Jill had broken her new record.

4   The teacher told the class that they could leave now.

5   The policeman asked Tim why his bicycle had no lights.

G   Write the story shown in this comic strip, using indirect speech.

H   Write these words and abbreviations in full.

doesn't   pram   who's   R.S.P.C.A.   Sept.   bus   A.A.
you'll   m   SW   U.K.   fridge

Synonyms

When we want to describe something, we have a choice of words.
We can describe a beautiful picture as **beautiful**, **pretty** or **lovely**.
Words like these, with a similar meaning, are called synonyms.
Here are three words and some synonyms of each.

active (adj.) lively, busy, energetic, bustling.

agreeable (adj.) pleasant, pleasing, welcome, nice, sweet.

amusement (n.) entertainment, fun, pleasure, game, pastime.

A Here are twelve words. Six of them are synonyms of the other six. Arrange them in their pairs.

tedious tight far gloomy tiresome melody

music dull dye firm distant colour

B Every word in the first column has a synonym in the second and third columns. Re-arrange the words in the second and third columns, so that the three words with similar meanings are on the same line.

Word	First synonym	Second synonym
absurd (adj.)	suggest	assist
perfect (adj.)	lazy	recommend
idle (adj.)	ridiculous	reverence
fright (n.)	adoration	inactive
serve (v.)	help	seize
possibly (adv.)	faultless	maybe
worship (n.)	perhaps	terror
advise (v.)	grasp	stupid
catch (v.)	alarm	ideal

Antonyms

Many words have other words which are opposite in meaning, called antonyms.

Examples: big – small   tall – short   open – shut

We can sometimes change the word to its opposite, in one of three ways.

1   Put a prefix, such as **non, un, im, in, dis, ill** (or **il**) before the word.

   Examples: nonsense   undo   impatient   incorrect   dislike   illegal

2   Change the prefix.

   Examples: ascend – descend   encourage – discourage
   increase – decrease   inside – outside

3   Change the end of the word, and add **less**.

   Examples: joyful – joyless   careful – careless   cheerful – cheerless
   harmful – harmless   faulty – faultless   tasty – tasteless
   brainy – brainless   noisy – noiseless   scented – scentless

A   Write the opposite of these words, using a prefix from the brackets.

   wind (un   mis)   behave (dis   mis)   poisonous (im   non)

   perfect (in   im)   obey (dis   mis)   sense (mis   non)

B   Celia is writing about her friend Jon, whom she admires. Change all the words in orange to their opposites, so that it sounds as if she hates him.

   I like Jon, who is tall and thin. He is a brainy boy, patient and cheerful in times of trouble, and always helpful and ready to help others. I play tennis with him and he is very encouraging, so that I play better. His bright and sensible manner always makes me feel good.

C   Write the opposites of these words.

   useful   sane   pure   certain   contented   legible   mortal   active   sure

D   Complete these sentences by using antonyms with the prefix shown in orange.

   1   An un ——— object is one not seen very often.

   2   An in ——— answer is one which is wrong.

Homophones

Some words sound alike, but have a different meaning and spelling. Such words are called homophones.

Examples:

Their means 'belonging to them'.

There means 'in that place'.   Their coats are over there.

Ewe means 'a female sheep'.

You means 'yourself'.

Yew is 'a kind of tree'.   You can see the ewe lying under the yew tree.

A   Write a word which sounds exactly like each of these.

vale   through   piece   rap   board   heard   knight   fir   tied   route

B   Write this passage. Find a homophone for each word in orange so that each one has the correct spelling and meaning.

Sam got a knew job as an electrician's apprentice last weak. The first day his boss scent him to work in sum old houses in the next town. Sam arranged to meat his mate Bob their after lunch but he mist the bus and had to run all the weigh up the rode. When he arrived Bob was just about to start. He reminded Sam that they had to switch off the mane currant first.

"You'll find the switch in the seller," he said.

Unfortunately Sam forgot to take a torch and when he had switched the currant off he could not sea the stares properly. On the third step he stumbled and his feat went from under him. It was lucky he had not gone any hire or he mite have hurt himself moor.

C   Mr Brown has made a lot of mistakes in writing his signs. Write them correctly for him.

BY HOUR FRUIT!
BYE NOW! PRICES HIRE NEXT WEAK!

BLACK
CURRENTS

GRATE BARGAIN
KNEW POTATOES

SOULS
HOLE FISH
NO WAIST

FLOURS
20 PENCE
A BUNCH

FULLY-GROAN
BEAT-ROUTES

FOR SERVICE WRING THE BELL

Idioms

An idiom is an everyday expression which says something in an interesting way. Instead of saying, "He told the secret to his friend", we can say, "He gave the game away" or "He spilled the beans".
Instead of saying, "She could not make up her mind which side to join", we can say, "She sat on the fence", or "She waited to see which way the cat jumped".

A   Match each idiom in the orange box with its correct meaning in the black box.

a nine days' wonder	to work on something without effect
a wet blanket	back to where you started
a white elephant	to get into trouble
back to square one	to boast about yourself
the lion's share	to be overjoyed
to beat about the bush	the greatest share
to be over the moon	a gloomy dismal person
to blow your own trumpet	to talk without getting to the point
to flog a dead horse	an unwanted gift which is a nuisance
to get into hot water	a wonderful happening soon forgotten

B   Complete the idioms below and say what you think each one means.

1   straight from the horse's ———

2   to be down in the ———

3   to turn over a new ———

4   to hit the nail on the ———

5   to make a mountain out of a ———

6   to strike while the iron is ———

Similes and metaphors

Similes and metaphors are expressions used to make descriptions more vivid.

A simile compares one thing with another, using **as** or **like**. There are many similes in common use.

Examples:

as black as coal

He runs like a hare.

A metaphor puts unusual words together to give greater effect.

Examples:

The bishop is a pillar of the church.

The cold fingers of fear began to reach him.

A   Write these similes in full.

1   as ——— as a fox

2   as ——— as a post

3   as ——— as velvet

4   as ——— as a church mouse

5   as ——— as a lark

6   as ——— as a lamb

7   as ——— as a pikestaff

8   as ——— as brass

9   as ——— as a cucumber

10   as ——— as a kitten

B   Write these sentences. Say whether the expression used in each one is a simile or a metaphor.

1   I feel as right as rain now.

2   The kitten has a velvet coat.

3   It's raining stair-rods.

4   The old man was as deaf as a post.

5   They came back from holiday as brown as berries.

6   The boxer left the ring with angry wounds on his face.

C   Find similes of your own to complete what these people are saying.

ITS AS LIGHT AS ——

THEY ARE AS LIKE AS ——

IT'S AS HARD AS ——

I'M AS WARM AS ——

Proverbs

A proverb is a short sentence expressing a wise thought in a few words.
There are a great many proverbs in the English language, which have been
passed down by word of mouth over the years.

Write down the proverbs which these pictures represent. Then choose five and explain
in your own words what each one is saying.

Prefixes

A prefix is a letter or group of letters placed before a word to give it a new meaning.

Examples: **un**important (not important), **re**write (write again), **im**port (bring in), **ex**-champion (former champion), **a**shore (on shore)

A Complete the words in the black box by adding the correct prefix from the orange box to each one.

un	circum	with
in	trans	a
post	mono	bi
sub	pre	
pro	dis	

—tony —pone —ference —hold
—pare —fer —agree —draw
—even —board —cession —due
—port —way —sane —doors
—cycle —safe

B Write words with these prefixes, and say what each word means.

im- un- non- anti- ante- vice- inter- contra- bi- mono-
re- post- circum- pre- pro- auto- in- ore- dis-

C Write this passage, adding a prefix to each incomplete word.

"My —cycle has —matic gears," said Alison.

"—sense!" said Helen. "I hate to —agree, but no —cycle has —matic gears!"

"Don't —dict me," said Alison. "I mean that I can change gears with a switch."

"That doesn't make it —matic," said Helen. "Now I can lock my —cycle to make it —movable. It's a —caution against theft. I'm afraid someone may —fere with it when I leave it. I think it's —safe if I don't lock it."

"Let's go —doors," —rupted Alison. "It's starting to rain. The weather —cast said it would."

70

Suffixes

A group of letters added to the end of a word is called a suffix. A suffix is used to give the word a special meaning, often by changing its part of speech.

Examples:

serve (verb) → serv**ant** (noun)

care (noun) → care**less** (adjective)

break (verb) → break**able** (adjective)

recommend (verb) → recommend**ation** (noun)

A Add a suffix to each of these words to change them into either an adjective or a noun.

envy govern wash fame beauty harm sense

assist enjoy brew frighten colour

B What are the suffixes in these words, and what do the words mean?

Example: hillock (suffix: **ock**) = small hill

clarify inmost bullock readable useless cigarette

anchorage distillery duckling careful dangerous

C Write a word with each of these suffixes.

-ant -ment -ance -ful -ling -ette -able -most

-less -fy -ous -ing

D Find an adjective ending with the suffix -less or -ful to describe each of these pictures. The first letter of each adjective is written for you.

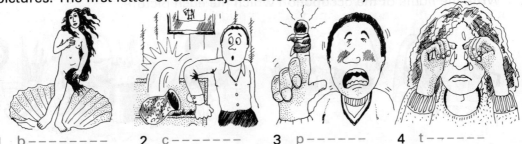

1 b _ _ _ _ _ _ _   2 c _ _ _ _ _ _ _   3 p _ _ _ _ _ _   4 t _ _ _ _ _

Occupations

Men and women work in a great number of occupations.
Usually the names of these occupations end in the suffixes **er**, **or**, **ist** or **man**.

Examples: a baker bakes, an actor acts, a cyclist cycles and a fisherman fishes.

A few occupations end in **ian**, as librarian.

A   Choose the correct occupations from the orange box to match the descriptions in the black box.

chemist	plumber
optician	doctor
florist	journalist
author	greengrocer
stationer	blacksmith
tailor	teacher
butcher	lawyer

sells writing paper, pens, etc

looks after your eyes

sells medicines

sells fruit and vegetables

writes articles for newspapers and magazines

mends water pipes

sells flowers

B   What are the occupations of these people?

1   She works in a library.

2   He sells groceries.

3   She sells tickets on a bus.

4   He drives a train.

5   She makes ladies' suits and skirts.

6   He fights fires.

7   She plays the piano.

8   He delivers milk to houses.

9   She uses a typewriter.

10   He sells newspapers in a shop.

C   Write the name of the occupation which fits each picture.

1   2   3   4   5

Think back

A Here is a passage from 'The Wombles Book', by Elizabeth Beresford. Write it out, putting synonyms in place of the words in orange.

Bungo's nose appeared first and then his bright little eyes and then his round furry body. As he was not very tall he couldn't see much except the tops of the bushes, which were laced with spiders' webs that glittered and danced in the early morning sunlight.

Bungo parted the bushes and edged his way between the leaves and grunted to himself as he made for the piece of Common which he was to look after.

B Write two synonyms in place of the words describing each of these people.

podgy   jolly   fierce   meek   glum

C Write these similes, filling in the spaces.

1   as ——— as brass

2   as white as ———

3   as dead as a ———

4   as hungry as a ———

5   as ——— as a daisy

6   as ——— as clockwork

7   as stiff as a ———

8   as ——— as Punch

9   as thin as a ———

10   as tough as ———

D Here is a collection of idioms, similes and proverbs.
Which numbers come under each heading? Make three lists.

1   to be over the moon

2   as cool as a cucumber

3   to drop a brick

4   once bitten twice shy

5   every now and then

6   a fly in the ointment

7   waste not want not

8   as silent as night

9   to send to Coventry

10   a miss is as good as a mile

Think back

E Write the opposites of these words using a prefix from the box.

connect   possible   lead   skilful   please

pure   roll   true   patient   selfish

trust   distinct   seen   like   active

un	in	im
non	dis	mis

F The opposites of these words are not made by adding a prefix. The opposites are entirely different words. Can you write what they are?

better   best   right (meaning on your right side)   false

right (meaning correct)   higher   inwards   upper   outer   shut

thin   heavier   nearest   costly

G Some of these words mean the opposite when you change the end of the word and add less. Which are the words, and what are their opposites?

joyful   happy   brainy   dreary   tasty   harmful   bucketful

watchful   spotty   colourful

H Under each of these people are two words saying what their enemies think of them. Write the opposites of these words to show what their friends think of them.

mean,   nasty,   lazy,   untidy,
cruel   envious   dull   spiteful

I Write this passage. Find a homophone for each word in orange so that it has the correct spelling and meaning.

The battleship left port for an aisle off the coast, at a speed of about ten nots. At the end of the crews it went along a channel following the boys which marked the root, in spite of strong currants in the see. It dropped anchor in deep water a little weigh off the peer. Small boats pulled by ores took the sailors to the jetty on the beech. The tied was coming in, and men on sure pulled the boats and tide them to the key side.

The mare welcomed the cruise of the boats, and took them to the Town Haul where they herd speeches of welcome and eight a splendid meal.

J Write these sentences, choosing the correct word from the brackets to fill each space.

1 The two girls ——— along the ——— on their bicycles, while Mark ——— up the river in a boat. (rowed   rode   road)

2 Barrie ate a bowl of ——— while watching the ——— on the television. (serial   cereal)

3 "I ——— that my friend Stella is ———," said Cathy. (hear   here)

4 We ——— the ——— of cows lowing in the meadow. (herd   heard)

5 Diane was afraid, and ——— not go through the ———. (wood   would)

6 The beautiful ——— had to be ——— to be believed. (scene   seen)

7 The ——— boys started ——— pull the rope ——— hard. (to   two   too)

8 Donna went to ——— some sweets at the shop ——— the Post Office. (buy   by)

9 I am still ——— after my illness and will not return to work this ———. (week   weak)

10 The wind ——— fiercely across the ——— sea. (blue   blew)

11 The ——— sailors ran to the ——— of the ship. (four   fore)

12 Aileen tied a ——— on the string so that the parcel would ——— open. (not   knot)

K What is a woman called who does the following?

1 acts on the stage

2 sells tickets on a bus

3 plays the violin

4 writes books

5 teaches in a school

6 looks after patients in a hospital

Common mistakes

There are certain mistakes which are often made in speaking and writing English. Read carefully through this list, and see if there are any you might make. One or two have already been mentioned on previous pages.

alright There is no such word. It is always written **all right**.
Are you feeling all right? All right, I shall go now.

among **between** **among** refers to more than two people.
The food was divided among the group of girls.

between refers to two people only.
Jan and Wayne shared the sweets between them.

beat **won** I won him at draughts.X I beat him at draughts.
I won the game.

beside **besides** **beside** is a preposition showing position.
She stood beside her mother. The house is beside the church.

besides is a conjunction meaning 'and' or 'also'.
I have no time to shop, besides I have no money. We took food besides drink for the picnic.

bought **brought** **bought** is the past tense of the verb **to buy**.
He bought a new shirt.

brought is the past tense of the verb **to bring**.
Have you brought your coat?

can **may** can means 'to be able'.
I can be there by two o'clock.

may means 'will possibly' or 'with permission'.
I may come if I feel well enough. May I come with you?

could **might** **could** (like **can**) means 'to be able'.
I could do it.

might means 'possibly but not sure'.
I might manage it.

farther **further** **farther** is used when talking about distance.
I am too tired to walk farther. It is farther away than I thought.

further is used when talking about time.
It is useless to talk further. I have no further use for this.

fewer less   **fewer** means 'smaller in number'.
There are fewer apples on the trees this year. I have fewer books than I once had.

less means 'smaller in quantity or value'.
Your share is less than mine. Meat costs less than it did.

from off   I borrowed a pen off my friend.X
I borrowed a pen from my friend.

from than   My writing is different than yours.X
My writing is different from yours.

help help but   Never use the words **help but**. Use **help** alone.
I can't help but feel sorry for him.X   I can't help feeling sorry for him.
I can't help but worry about it.X   I can't help worrying.

in into   **in** means 'in a position inside'.
She is in the house. The money is in the purse. The box is in the cupboard.

into means 'moving in from outside'.
She went into the garden. He drove the car into the garage. They moved into the house.

lay lie   **lay** is a transitive verb meaning 'place in position' or 'put'. it always has an object.
Please lay the parcels on the table. Lay your case down.

The past tense of **lay** is **laid**.
The hen laid an egg. She laid her weary body on the bed.

lie is an intransitive verb meaning 'to rest, stretched out'. It has no object.
I shall lie in bed.

The past tense of **lie** is **lay**.
I lay in bed. The cat lay on the mat.

learn teach   **learn** means 'to gain knowledge from someone'.
The class learnt arithmetic from the teacher.

teach means 'to give knowledge to someone'.
The teacher teaches the class arithmetic. She taught me how to divide.

like as as if   Do not say **like** when you should say **as** or **as if**.
Like I said.X   As I said.
It looks like it will rain.X   It looks as if it will rain.

But it is right to use **like** in comparing two things.
She looks like her sister.

Common mistakes

loose   lose   **loose** (verb) means 'to set free'.
We loosed the dog from its leash.

loose (adjective) means 'moving free'.
The dog is loose. The screw is loose.

lose (verb) means 'to mislay something'.
Be careful not to lose your purse.

negatives   negatives are words which give the verb an opposite meaning –
words like **not, never, hardly, scarcely**. Never use two
negatives together.

I shan't never be late.X	I shall never be late.
I can't hardly stand.X	I can hardly stand.
He wasn't scarcely able to work.X	He was scarcely able to work.

raise   rise   **raise** means 'to cause something to rise'. It is a transitive verb
and always has an object.
The men raised the heavy rock with crowbars.

rise means 'to get up'.
The sun rises in the East. He rose from his bed.
It is an intransitive verb and has no object.

The two halves of Tower Bridge are starting to raise. X	The two halves of Tower Bridge are starting to rise.

shall   will   See page 23 for the correct use of these words.

them   these   those   **them** is a pronoun.
We gave it to them. We have a letter from them.
Do not use it as an adjective.

Look at them birds.X	Look at those (or these) birds.
Them pictures are lovely.X	Those (or these) pictures are lovely.

try   try to   Do not use the words **try and**. Say **try to** instead.

Try and find the pen you lost.X	Try to find the pen you lost.
Try and find time for your homework.X	Try to find time for your homework.

Words which are not needed

It is very easy to use words which are not necessary when speaking or writing.

We may say: The plumber joined **together** the two pipes.
It is enough to say: The plumber joined the two pipes.
Joined means 'fastened together', so the word **together** can be left out.

Further examples:

He crossed **over** the road.
The fireman mounted **up** the ladder.

She shouted **out**, "help me!"
Where are you going **to**?

Now try these

A   There are mistakes in each of these sentences. Write them again correctly.

1   "I am alright now," said Vanda, "but I will go in the house and rest."

2   "I'll learn you to pull a face at me!" said Mrs Muggins. "You are a rude boy, like I told your mother!"

3   Donald said, "I am too tired to walk further. I will sit down on them stones, or maybe lay down on the grass."

4   "This strap is lose," said Gwyneth. "I will borrow one off you, or I may loose my bag".

5   "I can't help but feel angry," said Dan. "John gave me less plums that he said he would. Beside, I was going to share them between the three of us."

6   "I won Peter at chess," said Stuart. "I must learn him to try and play better. He didn't never have a chance of winning me."

7   "Caroline has fallen of her bicycle," said Alysia. "She tried to raise from the ground, but had to lay down again."

8   Tony said to his father, "You know that new shirt you brought me at the shop? Can I wear it at the party? It looks like it will match my jacket."

9   Enid went in the house to borrow some money off her mother. She said she would repay it back again next week.

10   The boys returned back from camp. "Camp learns you to look after yourself," said Robert, "and like the Scoutmaster said, you can't not help but feel better."

B   Write these sentences, choosing the correct word from the brackets.

1   Sidney certainly (might   could) do better if he tried.

2   I (shall   will) be going to Sunday School tomorrow.

3   Do not let the dog (lose   loose) from his lead, or he may worry the sheep.

4   The boys stopped, uncertain whether to go farther, but then decided to (continue on   continue).

5   Little Marion stood (beside   besides) her mother.

6   The task was too difficult for Ray. He (should   shouldn't) never have started.

7   "Just look at (them   those) cows, running in the field!"

8   Hilary's painting is very different (from   to   than) Lesley's.

9   She borrowed an umbrella (off   from) her sister.

10   He skidded, and (ended up   ended) in the ditch.

Some rules for good writing

In writing a letter, a story, a report for a newspaper, or an article for a magazine these rules should be followed.

1   Write in paragraphs. Start each new paragraph a little way in from the left-hand margin.
    The first paragraph should be an introduction, saying what the article or account is about.
    The following paragraphs should be the main account, broken into paragraphs of a few lines each to make the account easier to follow. Start a new paragraph with each change of subject.
    The last paragraph should be a graceful finish to your account, so that the ending is not too abrupt.

2   Write in sentences which are not too long. Use commas, if necessary, so that each sentence is easy to read.

3   See that all the rules of grammar are kept. These are the rules which have been described earlier in this book.

4   Make your account as interesting as you can. Keep to the main facts of the story. Do not wander about. Write in easy sentences. Use adjectives and adverbs to make the nouns and actions interesting, especially in story-writing.

5   Be careful of spelling. Always look up the spelling of a word in your dictionary, if you are in any doubt. Remember that there are no safe rules for spelling in the English language. Rules of spelling are only guides – there are exceptions to every rule, and you will not know or remember them all.

6   When you are relating what two people are saying to each other, put each person's words on a separate line. This makes the conversation easier to follow.

Styles of writing

How you write depends on the purpose of the writing.

1 **Advertisements**, notes to be written more fully later, information in gazetteers, and other long lists are written as briefly as possible to save time, money or space.

> **Example:** Newtown. S/c ground fl purpose blt flat. Double bdrm, lnge, fttd kit, bathrm. Gas ctl htg. Small gdn, own gge. 99 yr lease.

2 **Letter-writing**. The style of a letter depends on its purpose, and to whom it is written. How a letter is set out is explained on page 88.

3 **Writing a story or essay**. This should be made interesting, to make the reader want to read it to the end. Use adjectives, verbs and adverbs to make the account interesting and dramatic.

> **Example:** The little girl ran down the road to escape a storm.
> The same information could be much better written as:
> The little girl became frightened as loud crashes of thunder rumbled near, while she was still far from her cottage. She sped down the road while the lightning flashed, thunder cracked, and the rain came down in sheets.

4 **Poetry and prose.** Ordinary writing, whether a story, essay or report, is called prose. But if the writing is in measured lines, often with endings which rhyme, it is poetry. Here are the first four lines of Wordsworth's 'The Daffodils'. The endings of alternate lines rhyme, and each line has eight beats, or 'feet' as they are called.

> I wandered lonely as a cloud
> That floats on high o'er vales and hills.
> When all at once I saw a crowd,
> A host of golden daffodils.

Each line begins with a capital letter. All these lines have eight feet.

Not all poetry follows such a regular pattern. Look at this rhyme –

> Hickory dickory dock,
> The mouse ran up the clock.
> The clock struck one,
> The mouse ran down.
> Hickory dickory dock.

Try writing a little rhyme of your own of four or five lines.

> Geoffrey Mortimer Dunn
> Thought he would have some fun.
> He skated on ice,
> Fell through in a trice.
> No fun for Geoffrey Dunn.

Writing an essay

When writing an essay, divide it into three parts.
1 **The introduction**. Start by saying what the subject is. Describe it, and say what part of it you are going to write about.
2 **The main account**. Write your account in clear, simple sentences. Do not make your sentences too long. If the account is a fairly long one, then divide it into paragraphs.
3 **The finish**. End your essay in a suitable way so that the ending does not seem too sudden.

A Here is a short account of Horatio Nelson. It is written in a very few words in one paragraph. Write the account more fully in sentences, and in three paragraphs.

Nelson, Horatio (1758–1805). British Admiral. Son of the rector of Burnham Thorpe in Norfolk. Entered the navy at 12. Served in the Mediterranean Sea until he was 35, when he was made captain. Lost his right eye in 1794, and his right arm in 1797, in the French wars. Became rear-admiral in 1797, and vice-admiral in 1801. In 1805 he destroyed the combined French and Spanish fleets off Cape Trafalgar. Nelson was killed in the battle and was buried in St Paul's Cathedral.

B Here are some facts about the steam engine, and how it developed. Write an essay on the steam engine in sentences and paragraphs.

First steam engine with a cylinder and piston invented by the Frenchman Denis Papin, in 1690. Captain Savery patented a steam engine in 1698. James Watt patented an improved steam engine in 1769. Thomas Newcomen made a steam engine in 1705. Richard Trevithick made the first steam vehicle for hauling coal in coal mines, in Cornwall in 1801. In 1825 Stephenson made a steam locomotive, called the Locomotion. In 1829 his Rocket drew a coach along part of the Manchester–Liverpool line, at 30 miles per hour.

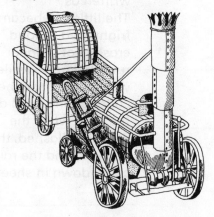

Stephenson's Rocket

Writing a story

The big difference between writing a story from imagination and writing an essay from facts, is that a story must have feeling and excitement.
In writing a story, try and give it as much atmosphere as possible. You can do this by your choice of words, by adding interesting information and by giving personal feelings and impressions. Writing a story is like painting a picture with words. The story should have a beginning, a main part, and an ending. Write your story in short sentences, and divide the whole story into paragraphs.

A Write what you think is happening to Stella and David in the picture.

B Write a story about a boy and his sister who call at a friend's house and see a burglar coming out of the window. What happens?

Exercises in writing

A Here is a story by Hans Christian Andersen, called 'The Real Princess', written very briefly. Write the story again, dividing it into paragraphs.

The Real Princess

Once upon a time there was a prince who wished to marry a real princess. He travelled far and wide, but although he met several princesses who were daughters of kings and queens, he found them all wanting in some way. They were not what he would call real princesses. Sad at heart he returned home. One evening as he was sitting in his father's palace there was a frightful thunderstorm. A servant came to the king, crying, "Your Majesty, someone is knocking and knocking at the gates and will not go away." "I will go myself and see who it is," said the king. The king opened the gates and was astonished to see a beautiful maiden, drenched with the rain. "I am a princess," she said, "a real princess. Please let me in!" The queen came up and looked at the wet bedraggled maiden very coldly and with a critical eye. "I don't believe you," she said to herself, "but we shall soon see." She went to a spare bedroom and took off the bedclothes. She placed a pea on the bedstead. On top she piled twenty mattresses, and on top of them she placed twenty feather beds. "Now," she said to herself, "she will sleep here and we shall see in the morning whether she is a real princess or not." So they put the princess on top of the twenty feather beds and twenty mattresses, and said good-night. In the morning they asked how she had slept. "Not at all," she replied wearily. "Not a wink all night! I seemed to be lying on some hard thing, and my whole body's black and blue. It was terrible." Then the queen knew that she was indeed a real princess. Only a real princess could possibly have such a delicate skin. So the prince married her, completely satisfied that he had at last found a real princess. And they lived happily ever afterwards.

B

Here is a passage taken from Arthur Ransome's book 'Swallows and Amazons'. But it has been written continuously, and not in paragraphs as Arthur Ransome wrote it.

Rewrite the passage in paragraphs. Remember that when two people are speaking to one another, you should put what each is saying on a new line.

As soon as they had watched Swallow's brown sail disappear beyond the Look-out Point and the north end of the island, Able-seaman Titty and the boy left the landing-place and went to the harbour. "This isn't a secret place," said the boy. "Any place is secret if nobody else is there," said Titty. "Besides, we are going up on my rock, where I was when I saw the bird that bobbed and flew under water." "Will the bird be there?" "I don't know. He may be." "Then it won't be secret." "Yes it will. Birds don't count. There's nobody on the whole island except us and the mate, and she's sewing on buttons. How many buttons has she got to sew?" "Dozens," said the boy.

C

Gary made these notes about the football match between the School and the Old Boys, in order to write an account for the school magazine.

Can you write the account for him, from these notes, in short paragraphs?

1 1st 10 minutes – School made strong attacks. A near goal by Smith – offside.

2 Old Boys counter-attacked but no goals.

3 Nil–nil half time.

4 2nd half. Strong pressure by Old Boys. Goal by Dawson (centre-forward) from corner kick by Wells. 1–0 for Old Boys.

5 Then half hour's even play. School left-back injured. Replaced by Dunn. 5 minutes before time Bridge scored for School after Old Boys' full-back slipped in tackling him.

6 Ref raised whistle to blow for time when School captain, Brown, scored lucky goal which bounced into net from crossbar. Result – School won 2–1. School supporters invaded pitch. Brown carried shoulder-high off field.

D

Write what happened in this incident from a golf match. Give your report in four paragraphs.

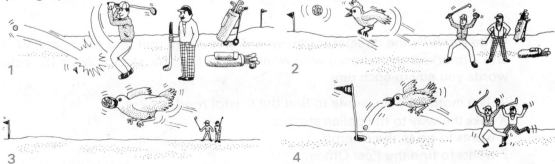

Exercises in writing

E

These three people meet and talk about their work.
Write their conversation in about a dozen lines, using direct speech.

road sweeper   nurse   fireman

F

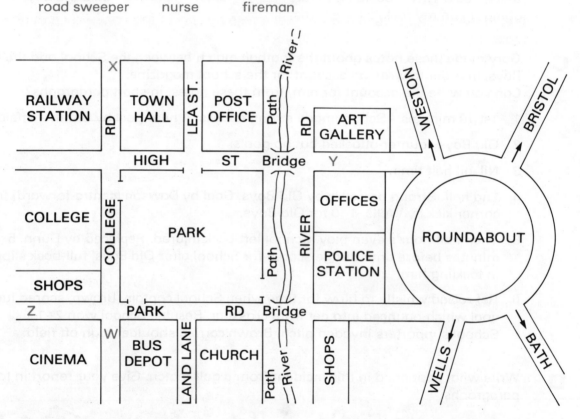

Write carefully the directions you would give if you met four strangers, W, X, Y and Z (marked on the map) who want to find different places. Write the actual words you say to each one.

W is a motorist who wants to find the Bristol road.
X asks the way to the police station.
Y wants to go to the cinema.
Z wants to find the Post Office.

G Here are the entries for last week in Kevin Day's diary. Write an account of how Kevin spent the week. Use direct and indirect speech where suitable. Divide your account into paragraphs. Make sure you use the correct punctuation.

Monday: stopped a little girl from getting run over, pulled her from the path of a fast car, her dad came later and gave me a football, said I was a good boy.

Tuesday: slipped on the road, sprained my ankle.

Wednesday: in bed.

Thursday: got up limping, saw the school match, to Harold's for tea.

Friday: doctor came, said ankle was O.K.

Saturday: baths in the morning, dad took us all for a ride in afternoon.

Sunday: late getting up, afternoon sunday school, evening by the river with mum and dad.

H Describe a vacuum cleaner to someone who has never seen one. Tell him how it looks, how it works, and how useful it is.

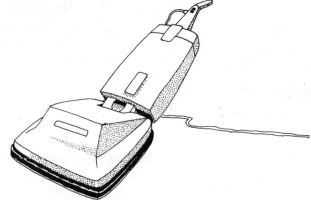

I Now you are a television sports reporter. In a few lines give a running commentary on the finish of the mile race at the Olympic Games.

Writing a letter

1 Write your address in the top right-hand corner. Put a comma after each line except the last, where you should put a full stop.

2 Write the date under your address.

3 If you are writing a business letter, put the name and address of the company you are writing to on the left-hand side.

4 Miss a line, then write **Dear Sir** or **Dear Jim**.

5 Start a new paragraph when you begin to write about something new.

6 For a formal letter beginning **Dear Sir**, write **Yours faithfully** at the end. Only write **Yours sincerely** if you are writing to someone whose name you know.

108, Sternhold Avenue,
Bradford,
Yorkshire.
1st November 1980

The Warden,
Westend Youth Hostel,
Holly Lane,
Keswick,
Cumbria.

Dear Sir,

My friends and I would like to spend three nights in your Hostel in June of next year. The dates we would like to come are from 19th–22nd June and there would be four of us, two boys and two girls.
Please let me know if this is convenient for you.

Yours faithfully,

John Roper

Addressing the envelope

1 Leave room for the stamp.

2 Start towards the left-hand side and write each line a little more to the right.

3 Put commas and a full stop where necessary, and begin each proper noun with a capital letter.

The Warden,
Westend Youth Hostel,
Holly Lane,
Keswick,
Cumbria.

A   Tony has been writing a letter to his friend Stephen, but has made some mistakes. Write the letter again correctly.

4 High St. Amblewick. 23 Oct. 1984.
Dear Steve. I am glad to hear you are coming to see us all on Monday next If you will let me know on which train you are coming I will meet you at the stayshun, all the news when I see you   Yours sincerely   Tony

B   Pat is applying for work at a clothing factory, after seeing an advertisement in the local paper. It is not a good letter. Can you write a better letter for her?

Flat 4A. Boston Crescent. Hilltown. 30 June 1983.
Dear Sir. I saw in the Hilltown gazette that you want machinists in your factory and that you will train them I am leaving Hilltown high school in July after I have sat for my exams and I want to be a machinist and need training can I join your firm I promise to do my best.

       Yours sincerely

       Patricia Hope

C   Pat sent off her letter, after addressing the envelope as below. The address was not well written. How should the letter be addressed?

The manager
the clothing factory
    Nielson and company
smithson street   Hilltown

D   Duncan Stewart is writing to the Greenbeck Photographic Company asking the price of some equipment he needs. He made some notes of the materials he was interested in, as follows:

1   35mm films for making colour slides
2   camera tripod
3   projection screen, 5 feet wide

How should he write his letter?

The English language

The English language had its beginnings in the languages of the Angles, Saxons, Norsemen and Danes who invaded Britain in olden times. Each time a new people invaded Britain, many words from their language would gradually become part of English.

English is mainly of Anglo-Saxon origin. The Angles and Saxons came from part of Germany, and Old English is in many ways similar to German.

The Normans, who invaded England in 1066, spoke Norman French and brought many French words into English. The nobles and many landowners spoke French, and French was used in the law courts for many years after 1066. Many of these words had come into the French language from Latin.

In the early Middle Ages Latin was used by scholars, and in the churches, all over Europe.

Anglo-Saxon, Latin and French provided nearly all the words used in English in early times.

Where do words come from that we use in the English language now?

It has been calculated that of all the words that we speak, write and read every day (not the number of different words), nine out of ten are of Anglo-Saxon origin. These are the common words like 'you, me, home, bring' which we use over and over again.

About one word in ten that we speak is of Latin or French origin, and we must remember that French words are often of Latin origin. Occasionally we use a word from another language.

Very few Celtic words, used by the early Britons, are in the English language, although they are often found in the names of places and rivers. The Welsh and Gaelic languages are Celtic.

Scientific words, and words describing new inventions, are mostly made up from Latin and Greek words – words such as locomotive (from two Latin words) and telephone (from two Greek words).

Here is a selection of English words and their origins.

Anglo-Saxon		Greek	Gaelic	Persian
am	why	arithmetic	cairn	caravan
book	you	diameter	loch	khaki
cow	young	electricity	plaid	orange
have		telegraph		pyjamas
house	**Latin, French**	theatre		
moon	audience	zoo	**Hindi**	**Spanish**
plough	beef		bungalow	alligator
pig	century	**Arabic**	shampoo	flotilla
run	decimal	amber		galleon
sheep	hospital	gazelle		
sing	mutton	sheikh		
sun	pedal		**Italian**	**Turkish**
they	pork	**Dutch**	bandit	coffee
town	religion	buoy	piccolo	turban
who	victory	skate	spaghetti	yoghourt
		yacht		

Just for fun

A   Copy this diagram on paper. Fill in the 7-letter words from the clues. Each word contains the letter T. The letters in the first column will spell the name of a country in North Africa.

1	T						
2		T					
3			T				
4				T			
5					T		
6						T	
7							T

Clues

1   A farm machine.

2   Completely, entirely.

3   A game in which you try to drop a ball into a net.

4   Immediate.

5   A cat may hurt you if it does this.

6   To copy someone.

7   A person who does daring jumps and leaps on ropes or on a trapeze.

B   Can you change the word care into the word bond, a letter at a time? It is done like this:

care   Each change of letter makes a real word.
bare
b**o**re
bo**n**e
bon**d**

Now change chore into spiny in the same way. The first word will be shore.

C   Can you make fifteen words from these letters?

a b c d e f

Just for fun

D   Copy this puzzle and fill in the letters from the clues below.

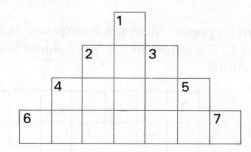

Clues

Across:

1   The sixth letter of the alphabet.

2   One of the two limbs from the shoulder.

4   Vapour from boiling water.

6   Guided a ship with a rudder.

Down:

1   At liberty, not shut up.

2   Had some food.

3   To spoil.

4   A short way of writing 'street'.

5   I myself.

6   The nineteenth letter of the alphabet.

7   The letter in the alphabet after C.

E   Here are five words in line.

f o r t u n a t e e l e c t r i c k i n g o t t e r s e n t

How many other words can you see in the line? See if you can find fifteen.

F   Change one letter in each of the words below to make the name of something found in a grocer's shop.

mice	butler	floor	spire	sale
toffee	breach	lord	baron	jeans
hum	ten	latches	mink	breed

Common abbreviations

A.1. – first class
A.A. – Automobile Association
A.B.C. – Australian Broadcasting
    Commission
A.D. – In the year of our Lord, e.g.
    A.D. 1980
adj. – adjective
adv. – adverb
a.m. – before noon (in the morning)
Anon. – Anonymous
Apr. – April
Aug. – August
Ave. – Avenue
b. – born; bowled (cricket)
B.A. – Bachelor of Arts
B.B. – Boys' Brigade
B.B.C. – British Broadcasting Corporation
B.C. – Before Christ
B.D. – Bachelor of Divinity
B.R. – British Rail
Bros. – brothers
B.Sc. – Bachelor of Science
C – Centigrade (thermometers); one
    hundred (Roman numeral)
c. – cent; caught (cricket)
Capt. – Captain
C.B.C. – Canadian Broadcasting
    Corporation
cc – cubic centimetre
cg – centigramme
C.I.D. – Criminal Investigation
    Department
Cl. – Councillor
cm – centimetre
Co. – county, company
c/o – care of
C.O.D. – Cash on Delivery
C. of E. – Church of England
Col. – Colonel
conj. – conjunction
cont. – continued
Co-op. – Co-operative Society
cwt. – hundredweight
D – five hundred (Roman numeral)

d. – died
D.D. – Doctor of Divinity
Dec. – December
dept. – department
do. – ditto, the same again
doz. – dozen
Dr – Doctor
e.g. – for example
E.R. – *Elizabeth Regina*, Queen Elizabeth
Esq. – esquire
etc. – *et cetera*, and so on
F – Fahrenheit (thermometers)
f.ff – (music) *forte* loud, *fortissimo* very
    loud
F.A. – Football Association
Feb. – February
fem. – feminine
Fr – Father (before a priest's name)
gal. – gallon
G.B. – Great Britain
g. – gramme
GMT – Greenwich Mean Time
H – hydrant
H. & C. – hot and cold
H.M.S. – His (Her) Majesty's Ship
h.p. – horse power; hire purchase
H.Q. – headquarters
H.R.H. – His (Her) Royal Highness
i.e. – *id est*, that is
in(s) – inch(es)
I.O.U. – I owe you
Jan. – January
J.P. – Justice of the Peace (magistrate)
Jr., Junr. – Junior
Jul. – July
Jun. – June
kg. – kilogramme
km. – kilometre
Kt. – knight
l. – litre
L – fifty (Roman numeral); Learner
    (driver)
lat. – latitude
lb. – (pound weight)

l.b.w. – leg before wicket (cricket)
Lieut. – Lieutenant
long. – longitude
Lt.-Col. – Lieutenant-Colonel
Ltd – Limited (Company)
M – one thousand (Roman numeral)
m. – metre; married
M.A. – Master of Arts
Maj. – Major
Mar. – March
masc. – masculine
M.B. – Bachelor of Medicine
M.D. – Doctor of Medicine
Messrs. – *Messieurs*, gentlemen
mg. – milligramme
mm. – millimetre
M.P. – Member of Parliament
m.p.h. – miles per hour
Mr. – mister
Mrs. – title of married woman
M.Sc. – Master of Science
Mt. – mount
n. – noun
N.A.T.O. – North Atlantic Treaty Organization
N.B. – *nota bene*, note carefully
N.C.O. – non-commissioned officer
N.H.S. – National Health Service
No. – number
Nov. – November
N.S.P.C.C. – National Society for the Prevention of Cruelty to Children
O.A.P. – Old Age Pensioner
Oct. – October
O.H.M.S. – On His (Her) Majesty's Service
oz. – ounce
p.pp. – (music) *piano* soft, *pianissimo* very soft
P.C. – Police-constable
p.c. – *per cent* (out of a hundred); postcard
P.E. – physical education
pl. – plural
p.m. – *post meridiem*, after noon
P.O. – Post Office; postal order
prep. – preposition
Prof. – professor

pron. – pronoun; pronounced
P.S. – postscript (written later)
pt. – pint
P.T. – physical training
Pte. – Private
P.T.O. – please turn over
qr. – quarter
qt. – quart
R.A. – Royal Academy; Royal Artillery
R.A.C. – Royal Automobile Club
R.A.F. – Royal Air Force
R.C. – Roman Catholic
Rd – road
R.E. – Royal Engineers
Rev. – Reverend
R.I.P. – rest in peace
R.N. – Royal Navy
R.S.P.C.A. – Royal Society for the Prevention of Cruelty to Animals
R.S.V.P. – Reply if you please
S.A. – Salvation Army; South Africa
Sen., Senr. – senior
Sept. – September
sing. – singular
S.O.S. – Save Our Souls (distress signal)
S.S. – Sailing Ship
St – Street
T.U.C. – Trades Union Congress
T.V. – television
U.K. – United Kingdom
U.N.O. – United Nations Organization
U.S.A. – United States of America
U.S.S.R. – Union of Soviet Socialist Republics (Russia)
v. – verb; *versus* against
V.C. – Victoria Cross
vol. – volume
w.c. – water-closet
W.R.A.C., W.R.A.F., W.R.N.S. – Women's Royal Army Corps, Air Force, Naval Service
wt – weight
Xmas – Christmas
yd – yard
Y.H.A. – Youth Hostels Association
Y.M.C.A. – Young Men's Christian Association

Index

The orange numbers show that you
will find information on that subject
in earlier *Nelson Grammar* books.

I = Book One
II = Book Two
III = Book Three
IV = Book Four